INSIDE FIGHTER

INSIDE FIGHTER

FIGHTER

Dave Brown's Remarkable Stories of Canadian Boxing

TOM HENRY

HARBOUR PUBLISHING

Harbour Publishing
P.O. Box 219
Madeira Park, BC
Canada V0N 2H0

THE CANADA COUNCIL | LE CONSEIL DES ARTS
FOR THE ARTS | DU CANADA
SINCE 1957 | DEPUIS 1957

We acknowledge the financial support of the Government of
Canada through the Book Publishing Industry Development
Program for our publishing activities. We further acknowledge
the support of the Canada Council for the Arts and the Province
of British Columbia through the British Columbia Arts Council
for our publishing program.

Printed in Canada.
Cover design by Martin Nichols.
Cover front and back photographs courtesy Dave Brown.
Author photograph by Carl LeBlanc.

National Library of Canada Cataloguing in Publication Data

Henry, Tom, 1961–
  Inside fighter

  ISBN 1-55017-266-2
  1. Boxing-—Canada-—History. 2. Brown, Dave, 1920–
I. Brown, Dave, 1920– II. Title.
GV1127.C3H46 2001   796.83'0971   C2001-910907-5

Acknowledgements

This book is based on many hours of interviews with Dave Brown and augmented with information from friends, family, sportswriters, boxers and promoters, and newspaper archives. Books that were particularly useful include: Murray Greig's comprehensive *Goin' the Distance: Canada's Boxing Heritage*; Michael L. Hadley's *U-Boats Against Canada*; Stephen Brunt's *Mean Business: The Creation of Shawn O'Sullivan*; Steve Neary's *The Enemy on Our Doorstep* and Jim Christy's *Flesh & Blood: A Journey Into the Heart of Boxing*. Former *Vancouver Sun* reporter and columnist Archie McDonald provided an excellent first-hand perspective on boxing in Vancouver in the 1950s. McDonald and Lorna Jackson thoughtfully commented on the manuscript. Additional information was provided by: Jim Kearney, Hugh Meikle, Norm Jorgenson, Dick Francisco, Don Majeski, Don McIntyre, Roy Cavallin, Mario Caravetta, the staff of the City of Vancouver Archives, and the extended Brown family. Sandy and Brian Kask's support made this book possible. Finally, I am indebted to Phyllis Brown for her patience, record keeping, wise suggestions and hearty lunches.

Chapter One

Dave Brown—feet apart, knees slightly bent—jabs his left arm straight out. From close to his cheek his hand flashes forward and twists. If it were to hit an opponent it would, in Dave's words, "snap his head back, keep him off balance." Dave has practised jabbing thousands of times. His legs move forward, always bent. His jaw is tucked to his chest. The jab is followed by an uppercut. Powered by the leg, buttock and shoulder muscles, it rises hard and fast. An uppercut can lift a man off his feet. If it makes contact with the pressure points on either side of the chin, an uppercut can temporarily paralyze an opponent.

There is no opponent. Dave is shadow boxing on the wooden walkway of a small-town New Brunswick railway station. It is spring, 1941. He is twenty-one years old. He is en route from Halifax to fight another featherweight. Whenever the Montreal-bound train stops, he jumps off for a brief workout. Tension is the boxer's enemy, constricting the muscles and starching his natural fluidity. Shadow boxing keeps Dave loose. A jab. Two uppercuts. A left hook. The locomotive's whistle sounds. Dave steps back onto the train.

He's clad in navy issue black leather shoes, blue trousers and heavy jacket. With a high forehead, wide-set eyes and full lips, he is compactly handsome. What's most noticeable about him, however, is his manner. He looks friendly, the kind of person you would choose to sit beside in a waiting room. Yet on the train he sits alone. Quite possibly the other passengers think he's deranged. Every time the train stops, this young man trots onto the platform and pummels an imaginary foe.

Chipman, New Brunswick. For five minutes, Dave works on his defence—"Weavin' and duckin' and bobbin'," he calls it. Straight punches are slipped by moving the head side to side. Bobbing the head is a defence against hooks. Gloves high, forearms vertical, a boxer parries punches, pushes them off course, blocks them to the outside. Dave's feet shuffle across the painted boardwalk. His head traces a route much like a pen scribing a sentence. He jabs repeatedly. The jab is as the scalpel to the surgeon. If he doesn't have one the operation is off. Punching and moving, punching and moving, Dave imagines his opponent's face. Roger "Iron Man" Dulude has a much-reconfigured nose, a famously hard jaw, intense eyes under a porch-like brow. He is known in Quebec boxing circles for being able to take a fierce amount of punishment, but from a previous encounter Dave knows he is a powerful puncher as well. Given the chance to wind up, Dulude, as boxers of the era like to say, can hit harder than a winter on welfare. One slip, a crack in concentration, and his opponent will be on Queer Street. White lights. Face up on the canvas. Out cold. Both fighters are rising talents and their rematch, at the Sir Arthur Currie Memorial Gymnasium, on the McGill University campus, is widely anticipated. Dave knows he'll be in tough. The jab can be a defence. It holds an opponent off. The whistle blows.

From the train window, New Brunswick seems to be a land of green. Tamarack. Pines. Sugar bush maple. For mile after mile the train passes through unbroken forest. The trees are not as big as the firs and cedars Dave remembers from his childhood in Vancouver, but the eastern forest is endless, mountains rising behind mountains like rollers on the sea. Meadows and streams break the green wall, tufts of fiddlehead fern emerge from the few remnant winter snowdrifts. Sometimes Dave catches sight of a woodsman, his downswinging axe a silver blur. Here and there on the riverbanks are settlements, little villages, each clustered around a sawmill and engulfed in woodsmoke and the heavy odour of fresh-cut timber.

Napadogan and Juniper Station, Bisson Ridge and Minto. Minto is home of the legendary Miner, a brawler whose teeth are all molars. Stopped at the station in Grand Falls, Dave notices faces pressed against the train's coach windows. He wonders if they think he's a German POW being shipped to an Ontario camp. Captured enemy seamen often have a preoccupied look about them, too. He's looser now, feeling limber. He slices the air with several well-delivered hooks. A boxer's style begins with his nature and background and emerges into punches and characteristics of ring behaviour. If a boxer is methodical, his style is methodical; if he is a showboat, his style probably is, too. Dave attacks with a flurry of punches. "I liked to work the inside," he'll say later. "I didn't piss around. I was always on the attack, moving in. I crowded. I was no cutie; didn't try to be a cutie. My best punch was a straight right-hand. And I could throw a good uppercut in close." It is a crowd-pleasing style, and he's amassed a winning record. In a fight in Montreal, he once overpowered an opponent in less than a minute. Dave's fists were pistons. His opponent tried to protect his body from the onslaught by dropping his arms, but that left his jaw exposed. Dave's *coup de grâce* was a sizzling right-hand that split his opponent's cheek. This style has endeared him to fans who like their boxing straight-up. It is honest, enthusiastic, energetic. The fight crowd calls him Davey Brown.

Were there experienced fight fans watching from the train—and there might well have been, for boxers could be found in every town and hamlet in the 1940s—they would have noted that Dave seems hefty for a featherweight. Traditionally, featherweights wear their clothes like a chair with a jacket slung over it. Dave has bulk on his 5'7" frame, a consequence of an insatiable appetite for the Scottish-style meat-and-potatoes meals of his childhood. He fights at the outer limits of the division—126 pounds. Once, when he showed up for a Halifax fight overweight, his handlers put him into a Swedish steam bath: 120 light bulbs in a plywood box, an early version of the Easy-Bake oven. Dave shed enough to make fight weight but felt like a wrung sponge. Before one fight in

Montreal, his handlers bundled him in two sweatsuits and escorted him to the furnace room of the Mount Royal Hotel. He lost three pounds in forty-five minutes. The trouble with this sort of treatment is that it leaves a fighter depleted. Without the energy to last several rounds, he needs to rely on a single punch.

St. Leonard, Ste-Anne-de-Madawaska. On the walkway at Edmundston, Dave lets go with a flurry of punches—his arms are so fast they could be connecting rods in an over-revved engine. There's something beautifully circular about boxing: to win you have to hit your opponent. To hit your opponent you have to move in close enough for him to hit you. There is no other way. It is a sport without freebies. To succeed, a boxer has to make himself vulnerable. That decision takes will and courage. You might win or lose, but the choice to step into the ring is what matters most.

The whistle blows long and hard. A jab, a right hook, and he steps back onto the train.

"I beat him," says Dave Brown. "A good fight, lots of punches. Dulude never was easy." It is spring, 2001. Dave, now eighty-one years old, is fiddling with a table lamp. Like a seed in an old husk, there is vigour behind his aging exterior. He is seated on a tan, shawl-covered couch in the den of his single-storey Port Moody home. Thin without being slight, he is clad in ochre slacks and loose cream pullover sweater. His eyes are blue and quick, his nose bashed in. A star-shaped scar marks the area on his forehead where most people have an eyebrow and his thinning white hair is combed straight back. His

His nose already bearing the signs of ringwear, Dave poses for a publicity photo, circa 1940. DAVE BROWN COLLECTION

head is propped on a chiropractic cushion that resembles a snoozing lamb. A glass of water rests on a table beside him, a big-screen television rises in the corner opposite, and beside the television is a desk with photos of his four daughters and nine grandchildren. In the adjacent kitchen his wife, Phyllis, is sawing bread. The room's single window overlooks the overwintering survivors of a small, south-facing garden, a cedar plank fence and, soaring beyond, the spires of North Shore forest.

The scene is as unfussy as Dave's interests: family and boxing. For more than six decades his life has been braided to the sport. In 56 professional and amateur fights he won 48, 31 by knockout. During the 1940s and '50s he coached Vancouver-area boxers to BC, Pacific Northwest and Canadian championships. The most successful of these boxers, Len Walters, appeared in the British Empire Games, the Olympics and the US national championships. As one of the country's top referees Dave worked hundreds of amateur and professional fights, many for national titles. He chaired the Vancouver Athletic Commission during the raucous era of Tough Guy fights in the 1980s, and judged seventeen world title fights for the sport's pre-eminent organization, the World Boxing Council. About the only thing he hasn't done in boxing is traipse around a ring in high heels and a skimpy outfit, holding the round number aloft.

Dave adjusts the neck cushion and says, "This goddamned light is haywire." It flickers. A few more adjustments and it stays on. "It's funny," he says, placing the lamp on the table with a thud, "you don't remember the fights you won. It's the other ones." When Dave starts to talk his voice is raspy, but it warms to a deep bass. There is a pinch of Brooklyn in it. He speaks quickly and clearly, slowing only to wrap his lips around certain nouns: "Rocky *Marciano* was a beautiful man"; "We were anchored near *Wabana*, in Conception Bay." His opinions, like boxing, are endearing in their frankness. People he admires are "princes," they are "beautiful" and he "loves" them. He swears frequently, too, but not so much that the words lose meaning. When Dave calls someone an asshole or a prick or a son of a bitch, you believe him.

He watches few fights. Too many fighters rocketing from obscurity; too many coming into the ring after a trip to burgerland. "There is no use putting fighters in the ring when they are not fit because you are *asking for trouble*. Maybe you get a going over and you pay for it—maybe you pay for it later in life. I might be paying for my escapades—on account of catching too many shots at one time or another."

Dave can recall the names of fighters dating back sixty years. Telling a wartime story, he mentions making a phone call to Phyllis—collect. That was fifty-six years ago. To listen to him is to sense the crunch of gravel on a St. John's path, the clammy mould of a north-facing Glasgow tenement wall, the drumbeat of a fist-driven speed bag. If he has lost any of his wits, which seems doubtful, he must have begun life with plenty.

Phyllis calls that lunch is ready. She's an attractive woman, with a broad, smooth face and greying hair. Once a top athlete, she still golfs and walks regularly and looks strong and healthy. She doesn't drink tea or coffee because she doesn't like the taste. Dave heaves himself

Boxing was popular in Montreal when Dave left the Crescent Athletic Club and joined the navy. His return to the city in 1941 as a services boxer was occasion for a lot of press hoopla.

off the couch and makes his way to the kitchen table. He suffers from dizziness and supports himself with a hand on the wall. There is no frailty in his appetite. As he spoons up a lunch of homemade chicken soup, sliced red tomatoes and fresh bread, he and Phyllis, whom Dave calls Phyll, chat about boxing promoters. They are both fast talkers, keen, and the names come quickly. When Dave wants to emphasize a point he will grab a listener by the arm, his fingers separating the triceps from the bone. His clasp is hard enough to squeeze the juice from a green apple. He and Phyllis also like to back up stories with evidence. From a spare room they fetch awards, photos, medallions: Dave's induction papers from the Canadian Boxing Hall of Fame, the City of Vancouver Civic Merit Award. Even Dave's personal phone book is retrieved. Black, with lined paper, it contains the names and phone numbers of a half century of boxing greats. Joe Frazier's phone number is there, as is Sugar Ray Leonard's and the numbers of dozens of prominent boxers. Dave knows these people. He's associated with Don King, Mike Tyson, Jimmy McLarnin. They are a community linked by boxing. Posters, trophies, autographs spill across the table. Dave's life has included so many folds that it surprises even himself. Spotting an aging business card he says, "What the hell is this?" Then he remembers and a story surfaces. The memorabilia of a lifetime in boxing takes many shapes. From a cupboard emerges a pair of miniature boxing gloves, signed by so many champions that it would be easier to list those left off. "What about the shorts, Phyll," asks Dave. "Where are the shorts?" "Oh, the shorts," says Phyllis, setting her sandwich aside and disappearing around two corners into their bedroom. "You haven't seen the shorts?" says Dave incredulously.

Her eyes vivid with anticipation, Phyllis emerges with a plain paper bag. "The blood is gone," says Dave, reaching in. "You know who wore these, don't you? Now that was a fight."

Chapter Two

Hours before the May, 1972, heavyweight match between Canadian George Chuvalo and Muhammad Ali, Dave Brown strode into the bedroom of his home at 4280 Venables Street in Burnaby and laid a black kit bag on the bed. From a dresser he took a pair of black trousers and folded them into the kit. He added underwear, a short-sleeved white cotton shirt, and a black bow tie. Beside these he placed his boxing shoes, a pair of black Everlasts, size eight. "Boxing shoes are light," Dave says. "They let you pivot, twist and turn. I knew that I was going to have to work. Reffing a guy like Ali isn't easy. You move. You sweat. I knew this guy."

Dave first met Muhammad Ali in January, when the then ex-heavyweight champion fought two five-round exhibitions at the Pacific Coliseum in a warm-up for several Canadian title bouts. As Vancouver's leading professional boxing referee, Dave was asked to work both fights. "As is often the case in Vancouver, the promoters didn't know their ass from a hole in the ground about boxing," he recalls. "When I said I'd just had a hernia operation, they said, 'Don't worry. Ali will only go one round with each of his opponents.' I said, 'Are you kidding? They'll bring in a big tub of shit, give Ali a workout, then they'll bring in a speedball. They'll both go five rounds!'" He agreed to split the refereeing duties with former boxer and long-time fight enthusiast, Doug Powell.

It was Powell's misfortune to draw the first half of the exhibition, a sorry five rounder featuring the barge-like Tracey Summerfield. At 290 pounds, Summerfield would have provided little challenge for even a basement-ranked boxer, but against the nimble Ali he was reduced to the status of a mobile punching bag. Heaving and grunting, he thrust his stubby arms out in vain at his dancing opponent, his punches always arriving a split second late. It wasn't so much an exhibition as it was a workout, and the disgruntled fans booed and hissed until the last fist on flab finished the fifth round. While Ali awaited his second opponent, a relieved Powell traded places with Dave at ringside, adding as they passed that Ali had a ruse planned for Dave. "He said Ali and this other guy were going to work me into a corner. I thought, 'Horseshit! I'm not going to look like an asshole in front of my hometown.'"

So from the moment wiry Jeff Merritt stepped into the ring the fans watched a kind of double fight—two top-ranked boxers duking it out and trying to corner a wary fifty-two-year-old referee. Merritt, once ranked fifth in the world, had a superb jab and good balance. Instead of waiting for Ali as Summerfield had done, Merritt moved in, clearing the way with his left, then sweeping in with straight rights and uppercuts. Ali responded by getting up onto the balls of his feet, hitting Merritt with a flurry of quick combinations, then bouncing away. Neither boxer was loading his punches as he would in a real fight, of course, but at least they put on a legitimate exhibition of skills. Yet for all their wheeling and shifting, they couldn't close Dave in. He weaved and spun away, always waiting until the last second before eluding the trap. After four rounds of unsuccessfully trying to dance Dave into a corner, Merritt dropped his gloves in a gesture of surrender and said to Ali, "We're not going to catch this guy!"

The exhibition was a success. In February, 1972, promoters Nick Zubray and Murray Pezim signed Ali and Chuvalo to a real fight. Dubbed "The Second Reckoning," the match was the biggest name, biggest purse fight staged in Canada, with a quarter of a million dollars in contracts and an audience of fifty million people in thirty-four countries.

Until 1972, name fighters appeared in BC only as entertainers. In the early 1930s, former heavyweight champion Jack Dempsey toyed with several locals in exhibitions at the Calvary Club, one of a dozen dingy fight joints in Vancouver. A few years later, Max Baer stepped into the Denman Arena to face an unknown, James J. Walsh. Boldly billed as "the Alberta Assassin," Walsh lasted one punch. Joe Louis, "the Brown Bomber," fought exhibitions in Vancouver and Victoria. So did champions Willie Pep and Archie Moore.

The 1909 Vancouver fight between heavyweight

champion Jack Johnson and longshoreman and sometime actor Victor McLaglen was neither entertaining nor important at the time, but has since achieved sideways relevance in boxing history. Johnson, a black American with a preference—scandalous at the time—for fancy hotels and white women, had just arrived from Australia where he had thrashed Tommy Burns, a Canadian and holder of the world white heavyweight title, in a world heavyweight championship. Not only did his victory open the most lucrative and celebrated title in all of sports to black athletes, but the way he fought—taunting Burns, joking with the crowd—imposed on the staid institution of boxing the cult of personality, the idea that a boxer's character might be as great a weapon as fists. Before Johnson took the title, boxing was firmly identified with two kinds of men: supposedly stoic, healthy-living whites like Burns and his predecessor, the mighty John L. Sullivan, both of whom modelled themselves on the heroic Greek boxers of ancient times; or black fighters, like Nova Scotia's remarkable Sam Langford, who never spoke out when he was promoted as "the Boston Tar Baby," never complained when his accomplishments were attributed not to his considerable discipline and devotion but to the thickness of his skull. Mouthy, black and good, Jack Johnson was so singular that boxing would not see his like for half a century.

In Vancouver, McLaglen was beaten so thoroughly by Johnson that he abandoned any hope of succeeding in the sport and lit out for Hollywood instead, where he later won a best actor Academy Award for his performance in the 1935 thriller, *The Informer*. In 1955, an aging Tommy

Burns arrived in Vancouver, but by then the fight was gone from him. An emissary of a sect that preached universal love, Burns had just finished a spiritual revival when he collapsed and died at a Granville Street home, just two miles from the site of the Ali–Chuvalo fight.

If a boxing match is to be more than a demonstration of ring skills something of value has to be at stake. Usually it's a ranking with a boxing organization. The higher the ranking, the greater the recognition. For professional boxers, recognition equals money. Sometimes boxers forget about rankings and fight hard and well because they don't like their opponent, or don't like something their opponent did or said. In these grudge matches character is ventured. In the best fights, character *and* ranking— pride and money—are at stake.

In a fifteen-round fight in Toronto in 1966, Muhammad Ali beat and humiliated George Chuvalo. Ali, then twenty-three years old, danced around the lumbering Canadian, jabbing and punching like a boy teasing a tethered dog. All Chuvalo got in were a few low blows, but they caused Ali to urinate blood for weeks. He said Chuvalo was the dirtiest fighter he'd ever encountered.

Ali had been fighting since age twelve. Angered by the theft of a bicycle, Cassius Clay, as he was then known, trotted into a gymnasium in his native Louisville and, peering up at the cop who ran the place, said he wanted to take care of himself. Under the guidance of several excellent trainers he developed his loose-limbed, herky-jerky style. He was good, knew it, and told everyone he would one day be champion. When he was seventeen, he asked professional trainer Angelo Dundee to let him spar with Dundee's top fighter, Willie Pastrano, a seasoned fighter with eight years' experience and a 48–12 record. At first Dundee refused, but Clay persisted. In a later reminiscence with sports writer Dave Anderson, Dundee recalled what happened: "Lo and behold, as soon as he got in the ring, he did a number on Willie, second to none. After one round, I told Willie, 'You're getting stale. You ain't going to spar no more. This is it.' Willie looked at me and said, 'Don't bullshit me. The kid kicked my ass. I couldn't hit him. He was too fast for me.'" Clay won a gold medal at the 1960 Olympics, then turned pro and, against 7–1 odds, beat bad guy Sonny Liston for the heavyweight title in 1964. Soon afterwards he converted to Islam and, fighting as Muhammad Ali, toppled the best heavyweight contenders of the mid-1960s. Prodigiously fast, an independent thinker, he was a beauty among beasts. He revolutionized boxing, doing for the sport, in the words of one boxing writer, what Marilyn Monroe did for sex.

Chuvalo's story, like his style, was more grind than great. The son of Croatian immigrants, he was raised in Toronto's tough Junction neighbourhood. His father, a cattle skinner on the kill line at Canada Packers, was so fearful of losing his livelihood that on holidays he packed a lunch and went to the plant to study his replacements. When as a teenager Chuvalo said he wanted to get into boxing, his father scoffed. Chuvalo took this as a challenge, quit school and started training. No one showed him how, but he was strong and persistent. At eighteen, he entered a local Jack Dempsey heavyweight tournament and beat four fighters in one night. He had a titanium chin and loved combat. "Boxing makes you something," he once said, "it's the purest form of sport. It's beautiful, it's brutal, it's the purest form of dominion. When I knock you out and I'm standing over you—right over you—it's the most wonderful feeling there is."

During Chuvalo's early professional career, that wonderful feeling was rare. After winning the Canadian heavyweight title from James J. Parker in 1958, he lost two of three matches, including one for the heavyweight title. He retired, returned with a new manager, and things improved. He beat respected Mike DeJong and a year later knocked out Doug Jones, at the time one of the world's top five heavyweights. Never swift or pretty, he wore fighters out with a kind of geological resilience. In 1972, *The Ring* picked the three most durable boxers in history. Chuvalo was the only heavyweight to make the list. Rocky Marciano, the great and undefeated heavyweight and a famously hard puncher, once watched Chuvalo, then said, "If it was a mandatory rule that a heavyweight championship fight had to go a hundred rounds, George Chuvalo would be the undisputed champion of the world."

After the Toronto fight Ali's and Chuvalo's careers diverged. Ali was soon stripped of his title and barred from boxing for refusing to enlist in the US Army. After three and a half years off, he lost to Joe Frazier in a one-shot comeback, then started a long, slow ascent up the rankings ladder, one fighter at a time. He arrived in Vancouver fresh off a less-than-impressive victory over

Mac Foster. A loss to Chuvalo and a big payday rematch with Frazier was over; Ali said he would retire.

During the same time Chuvalo—largely unregarded in the press—trundled along, strangely losing to fighters he was expected to dominate and dominating fighters to whom he was expected to lose. His record was 91 fights, including 16 losses and 2 draws. By 1972 he, like Ali, needed a good showing.

Ali arrived in Vancouver in late April with an entourage that included a public relations man, trainers and physiotherapists. He rented a gross of rooms at a hotel, seconded the Northwest Eagles gym in North Vancouver, and hired a fleet of limousines to commute between the two. Then he set about training. He gave the press some good quotes—"I'm perfect!"—but mostly left that to his aides. Trainer Angelo Dundee told a story about his devotion to family and religion. "He even has his own horse and buggy and when the horse gets tired he runs off with the wagon himself." It was hogwash, of course, but no one who saw Ali doubted that he could pull a wagon if he wanted. He was so newsworthy in every way that the newspapers couldn't figure out whether to put him on the front page or the sports page—so they ran articles on both. Columnist Allan Fotheringham levered an hour with Ali and later concluded that the boxer was, along with Pierre Trudeau and Chinese politician Zhou Enlai, one of the most remarkable men he ever met. "Twenty-nine ain't old but I don't want to go usin' stuff I need in the ring," Ali explained. "That's why I'm quieter than I used to be, not leapin' and foolin' around like I did."

Chuvalo arrived quietly with several handlers,

including manager Irving Ungerman, a few days later. Stocky, with immense arms, Chuvalo looked as if he were in constant pose, stomach sucked in. The cloth of his T-shirts stretched over his fifteen-inch biceps like the skin on an overripe fruit. His forearm was over a foot in diameter. At one time he'd been into jokes, too. After Ali called Chuvalo a "washerwoman," Chuvalo crashed an Ali press conference wearing an apron and brandishing a bag of soap and chased a stunned Ali around the ring. But those days were done. Both men were older and more serious. After his workouts, largely ignored by the media, Chuvalo strolled about town in jeans, jacket and a funny rain hat perched on his bony head at a jaunty angle. Gentle and big, he looked like a one-man piano mover.

On the morning of the fight, Dave met the two boxers at the Hotel Georgia for a weigh-in. Dave, peering from behind black chunky glasses, ran the scale himself. He was in better shape, too, having run every day for the last five weeks. Ali weighed 217½ pounds, Chuvalo 221. Both weights suggested a good, energetic bout. So did the boxers' attitudes. At an after-weigh-in press conference, Chuvalo said Ali had slowed during his layoff, that he was vulnerable when he didn't move. "Last time we fought, I had only seventeen days to get ready. This time I've had seven weeks and I'm in the best physical shape of my life. Ali isn't the fighter he used to be. I really think I can beat him." No one really believed Chuvalo, but his claim had a logic: as the next and final stage of Ali's quest for a championship rematch, he was scheduled to fight top contender Jerry Quarry; in a recent fight, Quarry had dominated Frazier before being stopped on a cut; in the seventh round of their 1969 fight, Chuvalo knocked Quarry out with a left hook to the temple. *Ergo*: Chuvalo had the stuff to beat Ali.

Acknowledging that no one had ever knocked Chuvalo out, Ali set himself the goal of flattening his opponent. "I want him out on his back, out unconscious, in the first round if I can get him," he told a crowd of local and international press. Then he glared at Chuvalo. "You've been on one knee, haven't you?" Chuvalo said: "Only in church."

With both fighters' careers at stake, about the only thing surprising when someone tried to influence Dave was that it came so late. As Dave was descending the stairs outside the hotel, a man associated with Chuvalo approached. "Davey, Davey," he called. "Remember, George is a Canadian. Anything you can do to help us, we'd appreciate it." Dave's arms shot up, as if he were held hostage. A lot of work had gone into the fight. He didn't want corruption, or the look of corruption, to ruin it. "Look, pack this shit up," he said. "I'm here to do a job."

A boxing ring with two boxers and no referee wouldn't look right. Yet a dozen hockey players might swirl around a rink and no one would notice a referee's absence. Golf is so self-regulating that many people are surprised when an official intervenes. But in boxing a referee is as necessary as the boxers themselves. The idea of two men boxing without supervision is a meal without a plate, a flight without an aircraft. A boxing referee works through the keyhole of regulations to keep matches from becoming brawls. He ensures boxers fight fairly. He watches for fouls. He makes sure that boxers are fightworthy and remain so throughout a bout. If a boxer teeters, gets cut, or loses focus, a good referee will notice. By calling off a fight that endangers a boxer's safety, the referee is acting as a moral arbiter for the sport. The boxers can slug away trusting that someone is looking out for them. The crowd, as they did on the evening of May 1, 1972, in Vancouver, can roar for a fight.

On Dave's mind as he paced the 20' x 20' ring in the minutes before the fight was: low blows. Chuvalo, especially, was known to whip in a below-the-belt shot while working the inside. As one of the heaviest hitters in pro boxing, his blows could do a lot of damage. Before the fight Sammy Luftspring, a former boxer and sometime referee who had flown from Toronto for the match, had a few cautionary words for Dave by way of the Vancouver press: "The first time anybody hits low, he better step in and be awful strong about it. Otherwise, it could wind up in a bloodbath or a kicking match."

The crowd had been warmed up by an entertaining match between two boys. Fighting in the fifty-pound class, locals Dale Walters (son of Len, Dave's star boxer of the late '40s and early '50s) and Barry Blatter had swung and slugged away at each other, delighting the crowd with their boisterousness. It was all the boys could do to hoist the big Everlast gloves chin-high, and when they swung the momentum carried them a half pirouette. The scene had some of the mood of Charles Dickens about it—with boys doing the work of adults—but it set a lighthearted tone for the serious fight to follow. When the boys' bout was finished the appreciative audience pitched so many coins into the ring that the two small fighters took several minutes to pick it clean.

At the opening bell of the main event, the fighters moved to the centre of the ring. Ali, in white silk shorts and shoes, took up his unorthodox hands-low, chin-out position, waiting for Chuvalo to make his move. Chuvalo, wearing purple shorts and white shoes, moved after Ali slowly, arms extended, like a man carrying an armful of firewood. "Flashin' and dancin' and stick-and-moving isn't my style," he had said. "My style: crowd and punch, crowd and punch and keep crowding and punching until something gives. Me or the other guy." The two boxers moved around the ring, Ali jabbing, Chuvalo shaking off the shots. The first round ended as Dave hoped, with a good pace established and the boxers fighting cleanly.

The second round opened with Chuvalo landing a right cross that snapped Ali's head. Ali responded with a two-handed flurry, then retreated. He fought as if getting hit was a blemish to his art. All the while, Dave moved and trotted to keep a view of the action, constantly talking to Chuvalo. "I kept telling him—especially in the early rounds—not to blow it. I kept saying he had a chance and not to blow it with low punches. I was just trying to con him into keeping his punches up."

At the end of the round Dave trotted to a neutral corner and pulled a card from his pocket. The fight was to be judged on the five-point-must system. After each round Dave and two judges would mark the winner on their cards. That boxer got five points. How many points the other boxer got depended on his performance. As well, the fighters had determined that a no-foul rule

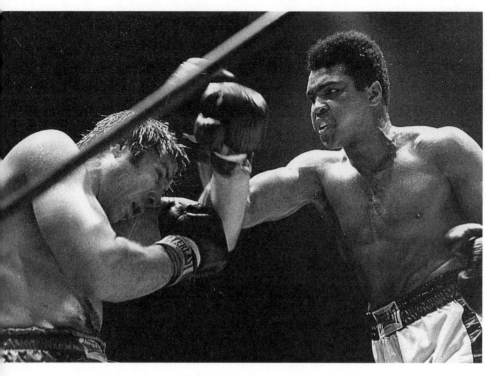

Despite an impressive showing in the fifth round of his 1972 match with Muhammad Ali, George Chuvalo was forced to rely on his famously hard chin to endure 12 rounds. VANCOUVER SUN PHOTO

would apply—meaning the fight could not be stopped and a decision awarded on a foul blow. And if a fighter was knocked out of the ring, he had twenty seconds to return.

Throughout the third and fourth rounds Chuvalo stalked Ali. Ali connected with numerous jabs, Chuvalo with fewer but harder hits. The crowd, and the experts, were surprised to see how well Chuvalo was doing. (Watching a videotape of the fight years later, Dave will say to a guest, "Chuvalo gave Ali a better fight than you

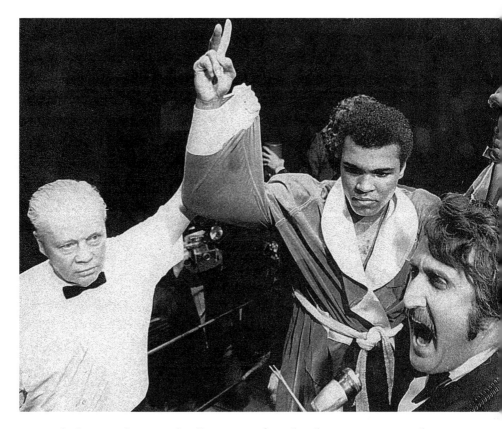

Dave hoists Muhammad Ali's arm after the boxer's 12-round victory over Canadian heavyweight George Chuvalo at the Pacific Coliseum in May, 1972. Ali's followers included ring announcer Shelly Saltman (talking, as always, right) who repeatedly declared the fight was coming from "the boxing capital of the world this night . . . Vancouvah!" DAVE BROWN COLLECTION

think." Then he'll turn to study the figures on the screen. "I had more hair then.")

In the fifth round Chuvalo surged. Swinging with both hands, sometimes inside, sometimes in wide arcs, he drove Ali into a corner. He pounded his body. In just a few moments he had turned the fight's momentum. He hit Ali again, backed away, his right glove poised menacingly. Ali dropped his hands in a "come on, come on" gesture. It was a crucial point in the fight—perhaps, it could be argued, a crucial point in boxing. If Chuvalo pressed the advantage, he could possibly best Ali. A few blows to the body, an opening on the jaw and who knows. Maybe he'd get lucky, like Henry Cooper did when he clocked Ali with a left hook in England. The punch hadn't knocked Ali out, but it sent him sprawling onto the canvas. Perhaps good fortune was on Ali's side.

From Dave's point of view, hand on the top rope, crouched to watch the action, it was Chuvalo's great chance. Later, Dave told Chuvalo what he saw. "I know, I know," said Chuvalo, "but I thought he was trying to sucker me into something." And Dave said, "You're right. He was trying to sucker you—sucker you into giving him a few more minutes to gain his equilibrium."

The round ended with both fighters ranked even in a straw poll of ringside journalists. But Chuvalo's opportunity had passed. Warmed up and now angered, Ali bounded out in the sixth round and snapped Chuvalo's head with a number of jabs. He followed with a furious assault that had Chuvalo teetering. The remainder of the fight was script: Ali swift and stylish; Chuvalo strong and durable. Dave remembers: "Ali hit him with every goddamned shot in the book. I think he eased off because if he'd tried to keep that pace he would have punched himself out." In the sixth, seventh and eighth rounds Ali orbited Chuvalo like a moon around a planet, his fists firing at will. From his vantage, Dave thought, "Chuvalo is trying to block with both hands. That's wrong. You block with the left, parry with the right." Chuvalo struck hard but not often. He was bleeding from a cut above the eye. His face was a bag of golf balls. He was marooned in the centre of the ring. He wanted to trap Ali in the corners but Ali wasn't going. Dave thought, "Chuvalo should be throwing overhand rights and uppercuts—that would work. Chuvalo's been coached otherwise. Ungerman doesn't know what the hell he is doing." By the eleventh round Ali had Chuvalo lurching, blood trickling down his jaw. His corner was screaming for a knock-down. "Be mean! Be mean!" shrieked Ali's corner man and confidant Drew "Bundini" Brown. "Squeeze out some of that beet juice! Work the cut! Work the cut!" Finally, Dave told him to shut up. Across the ring, Chuvalo's manager was also hollering. "Just last it out, George. That's all I want. Just last it out." The crowd chimed in, "Come on, George! Come on!" The twelfth round started with Ali lacing Chuvalo, but then Chuvalo came back and hit Ali with a right cross. It was too little too late. Chuvalo was still punching at the final bell.

Ali won a unanimous decision, but the fight satisfied all parties. No one seriously expected Chuvalo to win. But Ali failed to knock down Chuvalo, as he said he would, and in that way Chuvalo claimed a small victory. Both fighters benefited from their showing, Chuvalo pocketing $65,000, the biggest purse of his career, and Ali taking home $200,000. He was also one step closer to regaining the heavyweight championship. That the fight hadn't descended into a brawl was largely Dave Brown's doing.

Before leaving the ring, Ali told reporters, "That referee did a superb job. You might think it looked easy, but it's hard work keeping up with me for twelve rounds the way I was dancing and weaving." A few minutes after Ali left the ring Angelo Dundee fetched Dave. "Hey, the big man wants to see you," he said. They walked through a hallway, past a unsmiling bodyguard, and into a largely empty concrete-walled room. In the middle of the room several trainers were rubbing down a prone, towel-clad Ali. When Dave entered Ali sat upright and wiped his face. They chatted boxing for fifteen minutes, then Ali said, "Davey Brown, that was a good job. Do you want a souvenir?" Dave was thinking he might get a shoelace, but Ali had something else in mind. He scooped his blood-splattered satin boxing shorts from the floor and held them out. "You're pretty good for an old guy," said Ali. And Dave said, "I'm fifty-two years old and I used to fight as a lightweight myself."

Chapter Three

Dave Brown's father, also a Dave Brown, was Scottish-born to a branch of the warrior Lamont clan. In World War I he lied about his age and enlisted with the Seaforth Highlanders. Gassed and wounded in battle, he marked his sixteenth birthday in Chichester Hospital, then returned to the Front. According to family legend, his mother's reaction was, "He's made his bed, he'll have to lie in it." After the war the British government offered Brown, then a decorated veteran, a bread-and-water pension of thirty shillings a week. But it was conditional on unemployment; if Brown worked, payments stopped. As the younger Dave recalls, "My father sent them his medals and told them to shove them up the hoop."

In the early 1920s, Brown Sr. accepted a free passage to Canada in return for working on the prairie harvest. Leaving behind his wife, Mary, and their infant son Davey, Brown stepped off the train in North Battleford,

Saskatchewan. He discovered that Canadian English was comprehensible, sort of, but otherwise he might as well have been in the Belgian Congo. Farming and farm life—stooking hay, the itinerate threshing gangs, the reel and whirl of rural dances—were completely foreign to him. Some time in his first year in North Battleford Brown bought a twenty-five-cent ticket for a church lottery. First prize was a horse. When Brown won, the church officials drove him in a buggy to a pasture the size of the Isle of Skye, where horses grazed contentedly, and said, "Pick any one you want."

"What do you mean: 'Pick any one I want?'" said Brown, who didn't know a fetlock from a pastern. "Those are wild horses." That's right, was the reply. "Pick any one you want."

With the harvest finished, Brown took a job on the railroad. He lived in a plank-and-tarpaper trackside shack that barely slowed the howling arctic winds and did the jitterbug whenever a freight thundered by. As the thermometer plunged, so did Brown's spirits. The brief winter days vanished like thin-sliced bologna between the black slices of winter nights. He thought of returning to Scotland, or venturing to Vancouver. The issue was resolved one frigid, dead-of-winter evening when Brown woke fancying a cup of tea. He brewed a pot but drifted off while it steeped. The next morning Brown crawled from his cot to find the tea transformed into black ice. His son recalls, "That's when he decided to come west."

In Vancouver, Brown moved into his uncle's oak-shaded house on Little Mountain. If he hoped to find any Old World comforts with Bill Dundas, however, he would have been sorely disappointed. A big-shouldered, wide-open man, Dundas had embraced the frontier ethics of the rapidly growing city. He was a partner in a downtown blacksmith shop that manufactured machinery for the province's fast-growing farm sector. Located on Dundas Street, handily opposite a beer parlour, the shop was a dusty, cavernous structure crowded with forges and presses and redolent with the acrid smells of coking coal, fresh-tempered steel and human sweat. The business ethics of the operation were slightly darker than the carbon in the furnace flues. If Dundas got an order from an Interior dealer for an implement they couldn't manufacture themselves, he dispatched someone to the Fraser Valley for a midnight heist. Repainted, serial numbers rasped off, the implement was then shipped out for a quick and tidy profit.

The business of the family after Mary and young Davey left Scotland to join Brown was more orthodox. They lived in several houses—on Napier Street and on other nearby streets—before buying a home on 25th Avenue in south Vancouver. Simple and sturdy, it sat on a lot barely large enough for little Davey to play marbles knuckles down, but boasted an expansive view of the North Shore mountains. The neighbourhood, like the Browns, was a mix of Old Country values set upon a new land: Arts and Crafts homes with sheltered porches, often shawled in tumbling wisteria, were interspersed with towering Douglas firs—leftovers from a half century before, when Natives stalked the area for elk and Hastings Mill catskinners cursed logs to water's edge. A few of the Brown's aging, bandy-legged neighbours could remember those days, though even more common were families who traced their backgrounds to the hillside villages of southern Italy, or farming settlements of Gwangdong. During the 1920s and '30s, especially, immigrants from Italy and China, as well as south Asia, settled in south Vancouver and displaced the community's essentially Anglo character with an edgy, international complexion that made it the most dynamic, if not always peaceful, neighbourhood in the city.

While Davey was still in short pants, Isabell was born and the family was complete. Mary Brown, Scottish brogue boiling and soothing like a brook, ran the family. An outspoken brunette, with a sturdy frame and engaging smile, she boasted for much of her life that she was "five foot nothing." Actually, she was four foot, nine inches. Like her husband, she was of a well-known fighting family. Her father, Willie Hamilton, a stonemason, was one of Dundee's strongest—and strongest-tempered—men. Hamilton once boxed with a fighter named Jubilee Dan in the local quarry. When a friend objected to Hamilton's gambling, Hamilton stuffed him in a coal chute and nailed the lid shut. As a test of strength, Hamilton and several other Dundee strongmen were once pitted in a tug-of-war with a circus elephant. It is recorded that the men were besting the match—until the circus trainer cracked a whip over the elephant's tail.

By 1930 Dave Brown Sr. was working at the respectable, if poorly paying, Central Creamery. As Davey grew he became a part-time provider. On Saturdays he fetched balls for a wealthy old man named Waghorn at Shaughnessy golf course. He kicked back a dollar to his mother to buy the weekly roast and blew the remaining dime on salty popcorn and a movie at the Windsor Theatre. In fall he earned spare change selling apples he and his friend Sing, a Chinese-Canadian, stole from a neighbour's orchard—forty cents for a forty-pound box. Come winter he shovelled walks or, if there wasn't snow, sold holly pinched from a local front yard. "When you went to bed at night you had a holly tree," he recalls, "when you got up you had nothing." To save money he walked everywhere, thinking nothing of hiking from 35th Avenue and Walden to Hastings and Gore—a distance of approximately fifty city blocks—just to play soccer. If he was too tired for the trek home, he hopped on the deck of a passing truck. In 1930s Vancouver, a nimble kid could do that.

It was a difficult time, especially for Mary and Dave Sr., who were always digging in their pockets to find a few coins for the next meal. But as a new family in a new land, they learned to count on each other. Dave Sr., his gas-marred lungs forever wheezing, trudged off to work without complaint. Mary tended home and children on a budget that wouldn't keep some tony Vancouver homes in soda water. Dave Jr. earned extra money. Isabell, a life-long charmer and beauty, also helped as she grew. The bond between the mother, son and daughter was particularly strong. Live-wire Dave, forever barking a shin and skinning an elbow, needed Mary's stability. She was the lid on his kettle. "Davey," she'd say with the confidence of a Supreme Court justice, and he'd stop whatever he was doing. In turn, Mary enjoyed Dave's energy and noise, welcome counterpoints to the long silences and woeful stares of Brown Sr. Once, when Mary heard the bells of an approaching fire truck, she called for her son to come see. When Davey didn't respond, she called again. The truck was on their street and approaching fast. Still there was no sign of the boy. Only when the truck clattered by did Mary realize where her son had gone. Young Davey was waving at her from astride the rig.

Mother and son were fiercely protective of Isabell. Recalls Dave: "Once this neighbour kid, Harvey Wilson, pushed my sister from behind. She landed on her face. So I kicked the shit out of him. That night we had a party—we used to have house parties in those days, everyone would take turns making peanut butter sandwiches and a cup of tea or coffee. The kid's mother, Mrs. Wilson, said something to my mother. My mother was very outspoken. Very Scotch. She says, 'Mrs. Wilson, have I done something to offend you?' Mrs. Wilson says, 'Did you see my Harvey?' Then she calls her son Harvey, who was in the living room. He comes out with a big shiner. He looked like hell. Later, my mother told me, 'Dave, go play in another district, will you.'"

After ten years in Canada, in the mid-1930s, the family was no further ahead than they had been when they arrived. Dave Brown Sr., missing Old Country accents and pints, was for returning to Scotland. Mary Brown wanted to stay but relented. They gave the 25th Avenue house to a family willing to assume payments and sold the family possessions. The move, recalls Dave, was traumatic for both children. "It broke our hearts."

The Brown family's time in Scotland was more a sojourn than a residence—eighteen months. Dave's later memories of this era are snapshots: his father, wrapped in woollens, hawking kindling from a horse-drawn cart; his own job, as a nipper for Dundee's public works department, delivering spanners to ham-handed workers; his grandmother's little home on Glasgow's Rotten Row. One event does stand out, as much for its absurdity as for anything serious. Dave and some other youths were playing soccer—they called it football, of course—in Barony Street, in North Glasgow. The hard-luck area had no pitches, yet playing in the street was prohibited. Dave wasn't even playing, really—just jacking around—when the sound of a police wagon sent the other players scrambling to hide in the washrooms of the surrounding tenements. Dumbfounded, Dave stood his ground—until a big Glaswegian fist latched onto his shoulder: "Ya dinna run fast enough," said the burly cop. Two days later Dave received a summons. By this time the family had decided to return to Canada, and Dave intended to ignore the whole matter. But his mother would have none of it. Mary told her son that the police would track him overseas, clap him in handcuffs and leg irons, and extradite him to a mouldy Clyde-side prison. So Dave went to the courthouse. He thought the country operated on an innocent-until-proven-guilty basis. That was before they tossed him in jail. No questions, no explanation; just the clang of metal on metal and a turning of keys. Eventually he was released and escorted in front of a judge whose dour countenance summarized the whole impoverished, depressed economy of Scotland in the 1930s. "Were you playing on Barony Street?" he demanded. Dave, whose father thought *Canada* was a strange land, figured it best to be done with this bizarre situation. "Guilty," he said. The judge fined him two shillings—about sixty-five cents.

Muhammad Ali wanted vengeance for a stolen bicycle; Jack Johnson sought redress for his father's entrapment in menial jobs. Most boxers—prominent and not so prominent—trace their association in the sport to a childhood injustice. Dave just liked fighting. He enjoyed schoolyard dust-ups. His first official fight was on Gambier Island, under the green, summer-smelling awning of Douglas fir and western red cedar. The "organizer" was the United Church. A counsellor at the church camp pitted Dave against a Chinese-Canadian kid. They fought hard and quick, kid-style. Dave flattened the boy, finding in the competition—the high energy expenditure, the mix of fear and aggression—a deep satisfaction. "I kicked the shit out of him and I loved it."

The idea that this passion might twin with money-making did not occur to Dave until he was working in Montreal, where the family settled after returning from Scotland. In the mid- to late 1930s, the city was recovering from the worst of the Depression and jobs, if not abundant, were there for those who looked hard enough. Dave worked at a blue-collar job for Stelco. "Nuts, bolts, that sort of thing," he says. The job paid survival wages. "Boxing was a chance to make a buck," he says. "Of course I had to fight as an amateur first to get the experience."

Like all cities with a vigorous professional boxing scene, Montreal had a rising, self-sustaining column of amateur talent to draw on. The better its stars performed, the more people were attracted to the sport. The greater the number of amateur boxers, the better the chance of producing stars. The stars were siphons for amateur talent. It was through such a system that Leo "Kid" Roy rose, and Maxie Berger. A slick featherweight from the city's Jewish community, Berger was a superb fighter and is now remembered for once nearly besting the legendary Sugar Ray Robinson. Roy was a classy lightweight who dominated eastern Canadian boxers in the years prior to World War II. A fighter a lot of young Montrealers looked up to was Dave Castilloux, a lightweight who went on to become a top attraction at Madison Square Garden. There were any number of boxing clubs in Montreal, but the best fighters operated out of a converted office building at the corner of Crescent and Ste. Catherine Streets. To get to the Crescent AC (Athletic Club), as it was called, you opened an unmarked street-level door, hiked up a set of footworn steps, and turned right into a large room that was as remarkable for its simplicity as it was for cleanliness. In the centre of the room was a boxing ring and dotted around it were heavy bags and speed bags. A bank of well-scrubbed windows lined one wall and against another, between the hook-slung gloves and jackets and under a large clock, stood the club's CEO, prime minister, and unchallenged ruler: Russ Leighton. Burly and gruff, with the kind of experienced eye that can detect slackers and bullshitters at fifty paces, Leighton ruled over the club in a way that seemed stern in a stern era. "He told you when to breathe, he told you when to stop," recalls Dave.

Originally from Nanaimo, Leighton had moved to Montreal and set about assembling the largest stable of

Dave first got into boxing as a way to augment his income, but he discovered a passion for the sport that was to last a lifetime. DAVE BROWN COLLECTION

Chin tucked in, both arms working, Dave was a classic inside fighter. Here he is sparring with welterweight Harvey Dubbs. DAVE
BROWN COLLECTION

professional fighters in the country. He was hard and demanding and expected his boxers to submit best performances like factories expected time cards. But he respected his fighters, never belittled them or pitted them against hopelessly superior opponents, and that was a lot more than some managers did for their charges.

Leighton ran the club and arranged fights; the daily work of the gym he delegated to two lieutenants, Jimmy Symes and Solly Walman. Symes, who was black, and Walman, a Jew, were fire-and-water opposites in character, but made a superb training duo. Walman's style was non-stop, a staccato of hands-up, chin-down instruction that worked its way inside a boxer's head like a mantra. He knew everything and everybody in the business. From Walman, Dave learned to block body punches with the fleshy part of his forearm, to slip jabs with side-to-side movements of the head. Symes was more patient, a wise observer of the game who, after watching a boxer suffer through days of Walman's needling, would take the boy aside, prefixing his remarks by saying, "Now don't listen to that Jewish bastard."

Leighton's program was similar to a parent's rules for a toddler climbing stairs: when a fighter mastered one step of the program, he was allowed to move on. Dave says, "Once you got so you could spar, they'd put you against lighter guys, guys with a lot of speed. Then it was guys a little heavier or bigger, who could punch. Guys who could belt."

Fighting as an amateur featherweight, Dave soon established a reputation as a hard-working, energetic boxer whose style was at variance with the two usual approaches for featherweights. "Defensive fighters worked off an opponent's mistakes, waiting for a *break*," he says. "A fancy-dan was a stabber, a boxer who would hit and run. They didn't inflict much damage, but they piled on points." Many featherweights dance around their opponent, throwing jabs like spears, resisting toe-to-toe slug-outs. Dave's style was flat-out aggressive, that of what he calls an "enforcer." He worked close in, trading the risk of getting nailed for the opportunity to do the nailing. Such a combative style relied on physical fitness. He worked out regularly at the club, and increased his training to every night before a fight. Once a week he went for a twelve-mile run and workout along Lachine Road and the Aqueduct. "It wasn't just running, I'd weave, duck, bob. I was always moving, punching." During the week, on days when he wasn't in the gym, he'd often go for three-mile jaunts. Between his job, Leighton's tyranny, and his mother, there was no opportunity to get into trouble. Mary Brown did not exactly approve of her son's boxing career, but she wasn't about to ignore him, either. She watched his diet, monitored his social life. ("Sex?" he says, years later. "No way. My mother would never have allowed that.") One of Mary Brown's immutable rules was a tonic of hot water. Saying it was good for her Davey's constitution, she made him down a glassful every night.

Under Leighton's management, Dave fought all over Montreal. "You wouldn't know where you were going to fight until the day before," he recalls. He fought in Rosemount and Exchange Stadium, across from the Montreal Royals ballpark. For top events, like the Golden Gloves, fights took place in the Forum. Fighters came from all over Quebec, the Maritimes, Ontario, New York State. There might be thirteen thousand people in the audience. Golden Gloves were eliminations—lose once and you're out. To get into the finals Dave had to fight seven times.

After letting Dave understudy in the amateurs for several years, Leighton turned him professional. Fighting for little more than pocket change, he took on top featherweights from other clubs. One boxer he faced repeatedly was Romeo Ouimet. Ouimet was a tough featherweight fighting for the east end Champêtre Athletic Club. Their first match was an epic, with a controversial decision to Ouimet. The rematch became a fight of interest, with Montreal newspapers noting that a lot of money had been bet on the outcome. This time around, Dave did his work swiftly. After a brief exchange in the first round, Brown hit Ouimet on the cheek, splitting the skin like a tomato. He won on a technical knockout.

Dave's specialty was the quick fight, and newspaper clippings from the era read like a fast-forward film of boxing: "Dave Brown . . . finished off Jean Paul Desjardins in 1:45 of the first session of a 126-pound clash"; "Brown landed a hard blow . . . in the first round. Referee Deschamps would not allow the bout to continue."

He was quick on his feet, aggressive, fun to watch and good for the sport. Recognizing this, Leighton once had Dave fight an exhibition at the Crescent Club as an attraction to an upcoming fight card. He paired Dave with journeyman light heavyweight Paul LeBarron. LeBarron was a swift, skilful McGill University boxer who had a way of making opponents look foolish. Most troubling was his jab, which snapped out and tagged a chin like a frog nailing a fly, then recoiled. Dave knew he had to get on LeBarron's inside and for the first three rounds he succeeded. "I was having a ball," recalls Dave. "I was kicking the shit out of him. Because once I got inside, I could work with both hands."

Some months before, a journeyman professional lightweight had shown Dave a nifty move. "When a boxer was near the ropes he let himself fly back square on. Then you slingshot it out. And when you came out of it you led with the right hand. I had perfected it pretty good. So I tried it with Paul LeBarron. Well, Jesus Christ. He hit me with *his* right hand. If it hadn't've been for those ropes I would have landed in Ste. Catherine Street. As it was I came flying back and he caught me in his arms."

Twenty minutes later Dave was showering when he heard Leighton's gruff voice. "'How are you, Davey?' I said, 'Christ, my head is still buzzing.' It was the hardest I ever got hit in my goddamned life."

For young Canadian men, fighting was, and remains, an inevitable hazard on the journey to adulthood. If a young man is good with his fists, then the passage is smoother. The skills Dave picked up in boxing served him outside the ring as well as in. He says, "Most people don't know how to fight. They start in left field. By the time they are halfway through their swing a boxer can nail them three times."

Of Dave's half dozen street fights two stand out.

Scene One: A smoky St. John's dance hall, wartime. Sailors and soldiers whirl their partners to the big-band tunes of Glenn Miller. Dave, striding through the dancers, has just been told by a pretty girl that some lout wiped his hands on her new dress. He taps the lout on the shoulder.

Dave: What's the problem here?

Lout (standing up): What the . . . ?

Dave (to himself): Jesus Christ. I'm in for it this time. This guy is *big*.

Lout punches. Dave slips the punch, responds with a straight right that sends his opponent reeling backwards into a crowded table. A navy cop grabs Dave by the shoulder while the lout winds up with a haymaker. At the last moment Dave ducks. Lout hits cop. Dave exits.

Scene Two: Again, a Newfoundland wartime evening. Dave trots along the blacked-out waterfront, a flashlight illuminating the way over hawsers and rigging.

Voice: Put that goddamn light out.

Dave: Who's going to make me?

Sailor (emerging from the dark with a friend): I will.

Dave (stepping back and undoing his jacket): Oh yeah?

Sailor punches Dave, bloodying his nose. Dave removes jacket, hat. Two jabs, left hook. Boom! Right on the chin. Out on his feet, the sailor collapses backwards and hits his neck on the curb.

Dave (to other sailor): What about you?

Sailor: No.

Suddenly Dave is Florence Nightingale, offering to carry the unconscious sailor to get help.

Says Dave, "I never went looking for a fight, but I didn't back down, either."

Dave's day-to-day life in 1939 and into 1940 was austere. From work he went to the gym and, if there wasn't a fight scheduled, then went home. Women were definitely not part of his life. He was still under his mother's compass. Around younger women he was extremely shy. He didn't know what to say. His tongue, quick and energetic in male company, abandoned him.

Dave's sister, Isabell, was dating a handsome Montrealer named Jimmie Wells. When Jimmie appeared with an attractive young woman one day he introduced her to Dave as his younger sister. Phyllis Wells was a strong and athletic, with bushy hair and a clear, honest face. Their conversations were halting and awkward at first, but the more Dave saw of her the more he liked her. "She could hit a goddamned baseball a mile," he recalls.

Calm, confident, Phyllis was the second of three children. Her mother died when Phyllis was a child, and she was raised for several years by her grandmother. Her father, Findlay, was a conductor with the Canadian Pacific Railway and was often absent on trips throughout eastern Canada and south of the border. "I moved a lot as a child," she recalls. "It seemed like every year, and the same time—the first of May, when the leases came up. I couldn't tell you how many schools I was in. I know there was Verdun High. And Rushbrook."

Wherever she enrolled, Phyllis sought sports. She was a natural athlete, comfortable with anything to which she turned her hand. She was a forward on a championship grade ten basketball team, winning an MVP award twice, and played third base on the title-winning Verdun

Like Dave, Phyllis Wells was an enthusiastic and talented athlete. She was a star high school basketball and baseball player and a keen skier. Pictured here with female friends and Dave, she is second from right. DAVE BROWN COLLECTION

baseball team. At age seventeen, she was a key member of a senior women's team of more experienced players. She had excellent hand-eye co-ordination and played hard. When she started working at Northern Electric—the precursor to Nortel—as a typist, she was recruited to play in the competitive YWCA league. Even among older athletes she stood out and was selected to the all-star team. The city's sportswriters took note, praising the young star for her enthusiasm and "heads-up" play.

Besides baseball and basketball there was skiing

with friends in the Laurentians. They were a strong, adventurous gang, always looking to test their skills. Once, Phyllis and several friends took off cross-country from St. Adele, with the idea of skiing to a distant railway station to catch the homeward train. Across the slopes they coursed, stopping only to reorient themselves in the landscape. After hours of hard effort, they happened on a road. The driver of a passing horse-drawn sleigh informed them that the train was soon due, and offered to take them to the station. So with the girls hanging on the back he called the horses on. They made the train— exhausted, giddy—after what an adventurous young woman would consider a perfect day.

Athletics, then, was the common denominator for Phyllis and Dave. He was an attractive combination of live-wire personality and almost painfully shy boyishness. When they started dating he would arrange to meet Phyllis several blocks from the Northern Electric offices— for fear that he'd have to face a cadre of her female friends. He says, "I didn't want to meet the other girls. I blushed a lot. I didn't like talking to women." She didn't watch his fights but admired his athleticism and recognized his talent. For his part, Dave saw in Phyllis a strong, level-headed young woman who most enjoyed herself in sports.

Anyone seeing Dave and Phyllis striding arm in arm along a Notre Dame de Grâce street in 1940 would have recognized them as a couple soon bound for marriage. And they might well have been—if not for larger forces at work beyond the city's horizon.

Chapter Four

One day in the early autumn of 1942, a submarine slipped its mooring lines and idled away from the concrete pens at Kiel, on the Baltic Sea. Grey-black and sleek, *U-518* was of the latest design, with extended range and weaponry. It carried a crew of forty-three and a dozen torpedoes. The submarine was commanded by Oberleutnant zur See Friedick Wissman, a cerebral bachelor whose father captained German U-boats in World War I. Wissman's unique mission was, in the words of one chronicler, "charged with uncommon risk and adventure." It would also enfold Dave Brown in the war.

The *U-518* navigated the Iceland Passage westbound for the North Atlantic. The journey took fourteen days and Wissman used this time to imprint his command upon the vessel. The *U-518* submerged at sunrise and breached at sunset. In the daytime the crew slept to conserve air. He allowed the men the officially verboten luxury of listening to radio sets, but when an officer wanted to celebrate a birthday Wissman limited the festivities to two bottles of champagne. The crew called him *Wissmännchen*: Smart Guy. His orders were to search the waters of northern Newfoundland, then proceed to Gaspé Bay where, on the eve of a new moon, the *U-518* would deposit a spy, Werner Alfred Waldmar von Janowski. Born in Germany, he emigrated to Ontario where he worked as a labourer, but returned to Europe before the war. He was the submarine's sallow-faced passenger with the crescent-moon marks under his eyes and two oversized suitcases.

En route to Quebec, Wissman was to attack merchant shipping as he saw fit. *U-518* patrolled the Belle Isle Strait between the Newfoundland and Labrador shores for ten days in mid-October, 1942, but encountered only fish boats and what Wissman recorded in his log as a "completely dead area." On a tip from another U-boat, Wissman then headed east for Bell Island in Conception Bay. German intelligence knew high-grade iron ore was being shipped from the island's mines to Cape Breton steel mills. Five weeks earlier another U-boat torpedoed two ore carriers at the island's east shore anchorage. Reports indicated there were now more targets.

Running on the surface, *U-518* entered the broad mouth of Conception Bay at night and proceeded to the southeast shore of Bell Island. The island, egg-shaped and eleven miles long, is separated from Conception Bay's east coast by a narrow passage known as The Tickle. As Wissman glassed the scene, the only significant defence appeared to be a powerful searchlight sweeping from the island's ore-loading docks and across The Tickle to the Newfoundland shore opposite. Leery of open water, Wissman guided his craft close to the island. "We are deep inside the bay," he scrawled in his log. "So far have seen nothing." Nearer the loading docks, he spotted a silhouette against the high cliffs of the island. It looked like a ship, but he wasn't convinced. Then the searchlight passed again, and he clearly saw three steamers swinging at anchor and one at the dock. Lying in the shadows of the high cliffs, Wissman timed the searchlight's sweep. Every ten minutes—precisely. When the light passed again, he manoeuvred the *U-518* to attack. While his crew took battle stations he scrawled in the sub's log: "Moon comes out (as it always does when you don't need it)." Moments later he added, "Now is the time to strike." With the docked ship square and steady in his sights, he ordered the first torpedo launched. It was 3:30 a.m. local time.

In 1940, Dave Brown had little interest in the war. He had a job, a girlfriend, and his fight career was flourishing. He was patriotic but not mindlessly so. If asked to join, he would. Besides, the navy wasn't hiring. His friend and Phyllis's brother, Jimmie Wells, had tried enlisting and came back to report the navy was full and there was a two-year wait-list. Only news that Dave's father was going to sign up prompted Dave to reconsider. The army and air force did not interest him, but there was something appealing about the navy. He had never reefed a knot or faced down a southeaster—but there is rarely reason behind such passions. "I loved the navy, always have," he says. Dave Brown Sr. had said that if France went down he would join up. Then the newspapers ran photos of the German army goose-stepping into Paris. To appease his father as much as anything, Dave hiked to the navy barracks on Montreal's Mountain Street. He was going to apply and they were going to reject him, so he could go back to Dave Sr. and say, "There, I tried." The captain of the barracks was a fight fan. "Davey Brown?" he said. *"The* Davey Brown?" A few jots on a form, and Dave was navy. He would remain for four years and ten months.

To say that the organization Dave joined was in transition is like saying a detonating depth charge is undergoing a radical transformation. At every level, in every way, the Royal Canadian Navy was growing. From a force of two thousand men and fifteen vessels in 1939, it would boast 100,000 men and women and almost one thousand vessels—the third-largest navy in the world—in 1945. But in 1940, its obligations outnumbered ships two to one. It had Atlantic escort commitments, coastal patrol duties, a Pacific watch to keep. Rushing to expand, the navy made mistakes. Shipyards laid keels for vessels with incomplete designs, eager seamen languished in ill-equipped barracks.

The navy's low point came soon after war was declared, when two U-boats were reported sharking up the St. Lawrence. At the navy's Quebec City headquarters, officials scrambled to muster an opposing force. Desperate, they accepted the services of a "submarine diviner," a shady character who held a plumb bob over a maritime chart and muttered incantations. Two vessels were manned by army personnel brandishing pistols and

World War I carbines, and this less-than-awesome force was joined by an unarmed firefighting tug designated to drown a German attacker with a water cannon. The strange flotilla steamed downriver. They found no Germans but nevertheless holed the suspect dark with gunfire, destroying a river buoy. Given what it had to start with in 1939, the wonder of the Canadian navy may not be its role in beating Nazi Germany, but that it conquered its own ineptitude.

Dave lurched into navy life. There was basic training in Montreal, then a signalman's course. He learned the use of flags according to the International Code of Signals: twenty-six alphabetical flags, ten numerical pennants, and substitutes. He was instructed on proper operation of the Aldis lamp, the click-clicking of which became a Hollywood semaphore of its own in countless war movies. Then it was off to Halifax for more waiting, more training. All the while, the war moved closer. News of Canadian losses filtered through newspaper censors. Friend-of-a-friend accounts of stricken craft and hypothermic survivors passed from bunk to bunk. When the signals course finished, the class was divided in two: half were drafted west to British Columbia, half east to Halifax. One classmate joined Dave on the journey east. He and Dave were tossing a football around a Halifax park on a Saturday afternoon when Jimmy—Dave knew only his first name—got word he was assigned to a ship. On Monday he sailed aboard the corvette *Levis*. By Tuesday, Jimmy was dead—the victim of a torpedo attack.

In the spring of 1942 Dave was assigned as a signalman to the *Q078*, a sort of oversized, well-armed speedboat. Designed by the Fairmile Corporation in Britain, it was built of Canadian wood in a Great Lakes shipyard. Called a motor launch—or, properly, His Majesty's Canadian Motor Launch—it was one of more than a hundred built in the war. The Fairmile "B", as this generation was known, was 112 feet long, with a low wheelhouse and extended afterdeck. In front of the fo'c'sle there was an eight-pound cannon for shelling subs on the surface, and on the stern were rows of barrel-shaped depth charges. Powered by two immense gasoline engines, the vessel could make sixteen knots—twenty in emergencies. For eighteen months Dave's life was defined by the *Q078*.

The *Q078* and its sister ships worked best as general purpose patrol boats but were pressed into service as escorts. In their efforts to spread finite resources over infinite demands, the Canadian navy recognized two incontrovertible facts: the need to protect trans-Atlantic convoys and to guard vital local shipping. Since 1940, U-boats had roamed the North Atlantic at will, blasting hapless merchant ships from the water by the score. Every month brought them closer to Canada's east coast, where hunting off the entrances to ports was even easier. If critical coastal and oceanic shipping was to survive, the U-boats had to be stopped.

Tough enough to withstand the abuses of the open ocean, swift enough to chase a departing submarine, corvettes were assigned escort duty. Local shipping was assigned to the Fairmiles. Dave Brown and the *Q078* were charged with the task of escorting convoys carrying iron ore from Bell Island to Cape Breton. It was a journey of some five hundred nautical miles, much of it across the open waters off Newfoundland's eastern shore.

According to navy orders, the *Q078* was to log four days at sea, then four days in port. An escort was not to leave a convoy until relieved. That way, the freighters always had coverage, and the Fairmiles and their crew could reprovision. As much as weather allowed, it was a routine, and the crew of the *Q078* soon got to know each other and their craft.

Despite the navy's hopes, the Fairmile was not the ship for the job. As Dave and the rest of the *Q078*'s crew discovered, the sleek design that made for a high-speed craft was unsuited for heavy seas. In the open waters between southern Newfoundland and Cape Breton, in particular, where seas can challenge the largest deep-sea vessels, the Fairmiles ploughed and wallowed. More than once on the *Q078*, waves washed completely over the ship. In such conditions seasickness was endemic. The crew staggered ashore after a shift dehydrated and spent.

There were equipment troubles as well. As a submarine hunter, the Fairmile's central feature was its hull-mounted underwater detecting device—known as asdic in British Empire forces but more commonly known by its American name, sonar. Asdic was a ship's underwater ears. It operated on a principle familiar to anyone who has hollered "Hello!" into a canyon. Sound waves went out and, depending on what they hit, echoes returned. In the hands of an experienced operator—vised in a headset, eyes clamped in concentration—asdic could sketch a minimalist audio landscape. A resounding echo? An underwater bluff. A feeble return? A school of

Signalman Dave Brown poses in front of his sub-hunting Fairmile, the Q078. *After 18 months of sea duty he was transferred ashore and began training boxers.* DAVE BROWN COLLECTION

cod, perhaps. When an asdic operator detected solid echoes in motion, it was time to punch the alarm: submarine.

That was the theory. In practice there were drawbacks. Early models of asdic were fixed—they faced only one way. For the operator to get a 360-degree picture of his underwater surroundings, the ship itself had to sweep, like a man with a sore neck turning his whole body back and forth. In heavy weather this meant the *Q078* was broadside to the prevailing weather. Sometimes steep seas swept the entire hull-mounted asdic dome away. Even when conditions were calm the Fairmile's speed generated a cavitation that rendered the asdic almost useless. Paired with lumbering freighters, the ship sped around and around searching for submarines. As maritime historian Michael L. Hadley notes, a Royal Navy escort commander facetiously declared the Fairmiles most "useful in picking up survivors from torpedoed ships and transferring them to the nearest port."

Below deck, the *Q078* was not so different from the submarines it stalked. In their quest for speed, engineers had sacrificed beam. There was no room for hammocks so the crew slept in pipe bunks. Shorter than most, Dave was assigned an upper bunk, where the movement was the greatest. With the ship rolling, he could sleep only by bracing his legs. Even so, the bunks were fitted with foot-high bunkboards to keep their occupants from being launched mid-slumber. They ate at a tiny table, perched on their unpadded lockers, to the background roar of the howling engines.

That such conditions didn't lead to a miserable ship was largely a function of the men who crewed it. Twenty men jammed into a wooden envelope can coalesce into a team, or they can fragment into a multiplicity of grudges. At the centre of this crew was commanding officer Lieutenant John Finlayson. Of medium build, with box jaw and lively brown eyebrows, "Nory," as Dave called him, realized that the kind of "Yes, sir!" regimentation on larger warships was not always appropriate on smaller craft. He expected loyalty but was willing to forgive the occasional trespass.

With the ship running in heavy seas one night, Finlayson sent Dave aft to fetch something from the officers' cabin. The only way to this cabin was via the launch's exposed outer deck. Alone in the dark outside, Dave slipped on slick ice and crashed into a girder. He was nearly washed overboard. Freezing, wet and sore, he limped to the officers' cabin and had what can only be described as a small-scale mutiny. He lay on the captain's bunk. Then he rooted through the captain's things and dug into his store of candies. In his mind he saw the collective faces of a military tribunal, frowning and pointing to the brig. "Piss on them," he said to himself and stuffed a handful of sweets in his mouth. Just then Finlayson, wondering what had become of his signalman, strode in. Dave, mouth abulge, didn't need to plead special circumstances. "Don't worry about it, Davey," said Finlayson. "You just stay where you are."

As signalman, Dave was privy to information unavailable to the rest of the crew. He worked alongside the officer on watch, sending and receiving messages. He and Finlayson passed many hours together and a friendship developed. Once, during a heavy sea, Finlayson summoned Dave to the wheelhouse. A corvette nearby was signalling. Normally Dave glassed the ship with binoculars and said each letter aloud while the officer wrote the letter on a paper. When a word was complete, Dave flashed a confirmation, and the signalling continued letter by letter, word by word until the message was complete. Peering through binoculars, Dave began. T-H-E. "The first word is *The*. Got that, sir?" Finlayson had it. Brown signalled to continue. The next word came slowly. F-A-R-M. "*Farm*? I'm having difficulty, sir." Dave signalled for a repeat. "F-A-R-M. That's very clear, sir. *Farm*." The message continued. "THE FARM WOULD BE A BETTER PLACE THIS MORNING." Recalls Dave: "It was some bastard from the prairies. I said: 'Can I answer them, sir?' 'No,' said Finlayson, 'just ignore him.'"

The *Q078*'s second-in-command was Sub-Lieutenant Gerry Rising. From the Saint John, New Brunswick tea dynasty, he was well-spoken, always dapper, with the kind of understated aristocratic features you need if you are going to lug around a middle name like Easterbrook. Dave and Rising shared the same clothing size, and on nights ashore when Dave needed a natty outfit he hit up the generous Rising.

The rest of the *Q078*'s crew were agreeable, with one notable exception: the cook. "Cookie," as all navy cooks were called, was British. He was in love with the skillet, lusted for grease. He fried everything, and he fried it for so long that even a crew of young men could not stomach his food. It did not help that his stomach could not endure the rolling of the ship, and he was often seen throwing up. The crew hated him with such vigour that Cookie often locked himself into the galley. He opened the door for no one except his friend Dave. After an especially poor meal, Dave rattled the galley door. "Cookie," he called, "let me in." Dave found Cookie rummaging for his skillet. This time, he said, he was going to give the crew a real treat for their afters: fried watermelon.

Poor food and a tedious routine can lead a young man's mind to wander, and one day when his launch was at anchor in a Nova Scotia cove Dave's mind wandered to candy. He knew from a crewmate that there was a store nearby, with a candy rack the length of a man's daydreams. Finlayson was snoozing in his bunk, Rising fingering a book. With the stealth of commandos, Dave and his cohort slipped the ship's boat from the deck and rowed ashore. They marched for miles, fetched the goods, marched back and stowed the boat, uncaught. "We were heroes. We gave candy to everyone—at least those we liked," recalls Dave. "I had a lot of guts. I was a bit of a goofy bastard, too."

The crew were right in assuming Dave had special status with Finlayson. Dave knew when and how to approach the captain. Once, when a crewman wanted time off watch to see an overseas-bound girlfriend, Dave successfully pleaded his case. Finlayson said, "OK, Brownie. But make sure he's back by 7 p.m." Aghast, Dave watched the crewman stagger back to the dock, late, then flop into the guardhouse, and start spinning a revolver like a cowboy. Then the gun went off and blew a hole in drying underwear hanging from the ceiling. "He didn't give a shit," says Dave. "He was three sheets to the wind. His girl was heading overseas. It was my ass that was on the line."

Originally a fishing port and cannery, Bell Island became home to an iron mine at the turn of the century. First from shafts, then from an open pit, the island surrendered high-grade hematite, the richest ore in the British Empire. The cod-and-sail culture gave way to the industry of the mine. The local economy—centred in a clutch of buildings at Wabana—cycled to different rhythms than the other outports. People always needed food; ore they could do without.

The Great Depression of the 1930s crippled Bell Island's economy but rescue came from an unexpected source: Germany. As Hitler rearmed the country's military, the mines resurged. Between 1935 and 1938, employment at the mines increased by almost 40 percent. The last shipload of ore left Bell Island for Emden on August 26, 1939—two weeks before Canada declared war on Germany.

Allied strategists secretly ranked Bell Island as a probable target for enemy attack, after Newfoundland Airport but before the trans-Atlantic cable terminal at Roberts Bay and the city of St. John's. Early war telegrams between London, St. John's and Ottawa often refer to Bell Island as a matter of "imperial concern." As a first measure, the government of Newfoundland sent fifty police to guard the island's mine heads and landing piers. Canada contributed two guns and two searchlights. After the September U-boat attack, a Fairmile was ordered to patrol whenever freighters were nearby.

Behind the concerns about the submarines was an underlying tension about the allegiances of some Bell Islanders. For several years, there had been rumours that a family of resident aliens was sheltering an escaped German prisoner of war. The family owned a motorcycle with a sidecar, smoked cigarettes in a cigarette holder and trooped about in leather leggings—in the prismatic logic of war, sure signs of suspect allegiance. Short-wave radio sets were said to be installed in the homes of resident aliens. It was only a matter of time, authorities feared, until there was another attack.

After midnight on November 2, 1942, Dave Brown was aboard the *Q078* patrolling the black waters of Lance Cove, on Bell Island's southeast shore. Rising was at the helm; Finlayson was in his cabin. The launch was running an anti-submarine sweep, a systematic patrol designed to give the vessel's asdic operator the widest possible underwater scan. Anchored near Scotia Pier were three freighters: the *Anna-T*, the *Flyingdale* and the *PLM 27*. The *Rose Castle* was loading iron ore at the docks.

On a tip from the shore watch, *Q078* investigated a flat spot on the water. Nothing. There was another signal from shore: a submarine was in the beam. The *Q078* ran at full speed to the area, then slowed for an asdic search. By this time Finlayson was on deck, and he ordered extra crew to stand by. The operator picked up a few promising echoes but nothing definite. Too many wrecks littered the bottom for a sure identification. "We searched and searched," recalls Dave. "I guess we thought somebody was seeing things, or that they'd been drinking on the island again."

The *U-518*'s first torpedo missed. It whirred past its target, the *Anna-T*, passed under the stern of the *Flyingdale*, and slammed into the pier. The explosion sent ore carriers spiralling and destroyed much of the dock. Shock waves shattered windows in nearby homes and sent bedside clocks and pictures tumbling. Some parents thought the island was being bombed and dressed their children for quick evacuation. "Wham!" is how Dave describes the noise.

Quickly, the *U-518*'s Wissman selected another target. For twenty-seven years the SS *Rose Castle* was what seamen called a lucky ship. Two weeks before war's out-break, the sturdy ore carrier survived a collision in the St. Lawrence with a German ship dashing for the open ocean. Later, on the Bell Island–Sidney run, it was hit broadside by a torpedo with a faulty detonator. But that luck vanished when the *U-518*'s torpedo slammed into the *Rose Castle*'s hull. Moments later yet another torpedo hit the *PLM 27* broadside.

With no time to ready liferafts, many of the *Rose Castle*'s crew of forty-six scrambled into their life jackets and jumped overboard. Those who hesitated were sucked down with the ship. As the frigid waters rushed through the shattered hull, the boilers exploded, killing and wounding survivors close by in the water. Seamen struggled in the oily water. Dead fish and debris were everywhere, but in the near freezing winter water the hands of the survivors were too cold to grasp anything that might help them. One lucky sailor was dragged to shore by the ship's dog, a Newfoundland-like creature named Suzy. After hauling the crewman ashore, Suzy returned to the spot where her lifelong home had gone under. Most men could only hope that rescuers spotted the red lights that glowed from their life jackets. Or for a miracle. The night air was broken by men calling to the Blessed Virgin Mary.

It was not until the first explosion at the Scotia Pier that the crew of *Q078* had real evidence of a submarine nearby. Another Fairmile, the *Q053*, and a corvette, HMCS *Drumheller*, immediately went searching. It was a difficult situation, as they could not drop depth charges for fear of killing men in the water, yet to stop and pick up survivors was to risk being torpedoed themselves. The *Drumheller* searched farther offshore, the *Q053* closer to the island. Finlayson bravely ignored the danger and elected to search for survivors (a decision later deemed an error in judgement by military officials). With all hands on deck, the *Q078* trolled through the wreckage, its searchlight playing over the carnage.

Slowly they collected survivors. Exhausted from the cold, many men lacked the energy to even call for help. They were hauled aboard, blood pouring from their noses, ears and mouths. As the *Q078* idled through the wreckage the devastation of the sinking became apparent: flotsam, barrels, here and there a man. One sailor was flopped onto the deck. "Brownie," Finlayson called amid the confusion, "do you know how to take a pulse?" Dave knelt and felt the sailor's neck. "Oh, shit; he's gone."

The launch's light picked up an object—a body slung over a barrel. The figure hollered. He was black and feared he would be missed in the dark. Every time the light passed over him he screamed. He, too, was dragged aboard, then helped to Dave's bunk below. Dave fetched rum, rye and scotch from the officers' cabin. "These guys are cold," he recalled. "We got blankets and duffle coats and everything else and put it on them." The sailor in Dave's bunk had swallowed a lot of water. He told Dave he was bound for Halifax after this trip. He was going to meet his wife and two kids and take a holiday. Then he said he'd like a cup of coffee. Dave fetched a steaming mugful from the galley, but when he returned the sailor was dead.

The Bell Island attack has many postscripts, some big, some not. Military historians rank it as one of the largest wartime attacks on what is now Canadian territory. Of the ninety-three men who had their ships sunk from under them, forty died. In the months following the sinkings, an anti-submarine net was installed and orders changed so a patrol ship was on duty at all times, even when no ships were in port. The searchlight pattern was altered to infrequent intervals. Suzy the dog took up residence on the island and gave birth to several litters. The *U-518* landed the spy, Werner Alfred Waldmar von Janowski, near New Carlisle, Quebec. Janowski trooped into a local hotel, stinking of diesel, paid with outdated Canadian currency, and lit a cigarette with made-in-Belgium matches. Within twenty-four hours he was in jail. Outbound, the *U-518* torpedoed three more ships. In April, 1945, it was attacked south of the Azores by two American vessels and sunk with all hands. Nory Finlayson stayed in the navy until the end of the war and then joined Vancouver's Seaboard Advertising Company. Dave remained in touch with him until Finlayson's death. "I would have jumped in the water if he asked," he says. "He was a beautiful man."

When Dave Brown completed basic training in Montreal in 1940, he was transferred to Halifax and encountered a citadel figure he recalls as Musgrave—a burly, wide-open career navy man, who lorded over the jumble of sheds and parade grounds as if HMCS *Stadacona* were a flagship

Dave inherited his looks and build from his father but in character he was most like his mother. A talkative, spirited woman, Mary Brown loved parties and could dance late into the night. From left to right: newlyweds Phyllis and Dave, parents Mary and Dave Brown, and sister Isabell. DAVE BROWN COLLECTION

upon the seas. His charges were pseudo-seamen: they quartered in barracks dubbed "Forecastle," "Fore top" and other nautical names; they jumped to barked commands of "All hands!"; they scrubbed and polished so relentlessly that even the parade ground was spotless. The temptations of the city were a bicycle ride away, but under Musgrave's watch a seaman's life at *Stadacona* was rigorous, austere, disciplined.

Yet, as Dave discovered, Musgrave's interests ranged beyond traditional navy matters. Dave had just arrived at the base when he was summoned to the officers' mess—known by its nautical term, wardroom. It was an unusual request for a lowly signalman who did not yet know a protocol from an insult. He was ushered to Musgrave's table. "Sir," Dave confessed, "am I supposed to take off my hat or salute?" Musgrave rose and extended a beefy fist. "You can take off your hat in here, son," he chuckled. "They tell me you can fight." Dave didn't know what to say but that didn't matter. Musgrave already knew the answer. "How would you like to go to Montreal and fight Roger Dulude?" He briefed Dave on the details. There was going to be a fight card fundraiser, at Sir Arthur Currie Memorial Gymnasium at McGill University, for needy sailors. A Davey Brown–Roger Dulude rematch would be a big draw. Officially, the navy couldn't support the venture—that would be a bit of an impropriety, given wartime demands—but it would help however possible. Paid leave, train tickets. Musgrave finished by asking Dave if he was interested—and he was. But as the request was coming from a man who could find a lot of toilets that needed scouring, there was really only one answer.

And so, with Musgrave's covert support, Dave began his navy boxing career. He fought in Montreal, Halifax, New Glasgow, St. John's. He fought in rural halls and gymnasiums and in cavernous barracks, where the crowd sat cross-legged like school kids. It was a reprieve from the toils of base life but demanded diplomacy. Dave boxed for the navy; he wasn't a navy boxer.

The distinction took getting used to. Arriving in Montreal on the eve of the Dulude fight, for example, Dave reported to the highest authority he could think of— his mother. After dinner he and Isabell went to a Ste. Michele nightclub. While he was out, military police came knocking at his parents' house. Their badges and sidearms scared his mother. She thought her Davey must be in terrible trouble. When Dave checked in at the Montreal navy base the next day, he discovered why there was such a fuss. Many army and navy officers had money on Davey Brown and they didn't want him tanked out of shape on the eve of the fight. He didn't disappoint.

As long as he fought in front of appreciative fight fans Dave enjoyed what amounted to an extra detail. He never thought boxing was freakish—a spectacle to be jeered and mocked. Boxing required skill, its practitioners were brave and, if they fought well, the crowd should show its pleasure. The crowd's part of the compact was respect and appreciation. That was the arrangement and, until a particular boxing match on the Halifax waterfront, it worked. Dave tells the story:

> Jimmy Jones organized fights for the navy.
> He has this idea to stage a card on a ship. So

we bus down to Pier 27. There's a big, armed raider—the *Sarcasia*. That's a warship camouflaged like a merchant ship. There were guns galore. It was to sucker German subs to the surface, then they'd take over. Below decks there's a huge area where the ring was set up. Of all the ships in Halifax, all these officers had been invited to the big fight show. British navy, Canadian navy—all gold braid. Other than the guys working the corners and the announcer it was all officers. I beat a guy from London. Afterwards there was an announcement: "Would Canadian navy boxers report to the wardroom please." I said to Jimmy Jones, "We're going to get something." Up to this point, any time I got a trophy I sent it to Isabell. She had a shelf for them. So we got to the wardroom. They presented the Canadians with a palm-sized piece of bread with this yellow shit on it. And a cup of tea. I said to Jimmy Jones, "What the hell is this?" The officers had been so entertained. I was pissed. On the bus on the way back, I said to Jimmy, "You can shove those gloves up your ass. There's no way I'm going to entertain those pricks again."

But there was too much fighter in Dave for him to give up boxing entirely. Even when he was transferred onto the *Q078* he continued to box. He staggered ashore after four days or more at sea—weak of leg, stomach aching—and fought the next night. Between the demands of ring and sea duty, he was exhausted. Eventually Nory Finlayson, in conjunction with another officer, had Dave drafted out of the signal corps and sent to Halifax to become what the navy called a PTI—Physical Training Instructor. It was no small effort: at the time it was estimated to cost five thousand dollars to train signalmen. However, after much training, the PTI instructors discovered Dave had a major handicap. He couldn't bellow. In navy terminology he "lacked power of command," but it amounted to the same thing. When a PTI barked, they wanted a twelve on the Beaufort scale. Dave was a light breeze—a Beaufort 3. It was the equivalent of a sniper not having a trigger finger; a fighter pilot with double vision. Dismayed, he set about improving his chest muscles by working on the high horse, but it did no good. Dave could not bellow. His trainers gave up on the PTI classification and sent Dave to Newfoundland as a boxing instructor.

In St. John's Dave was stationed at Buckmaster's Field, on the hilltop navy base above the city. His senior officer was the base sports officer, Lieutenant J.D. McCormick, a black-haired, torch-eyed Nova Scotian. On their first meeting McCormick asked Dave about his plans to reinvigorate boxing. "What are you going to do," he wondered aloud, "get ships to fight one another?" But Dave already had a scheme. "You've got the US Army at Fort Pepperell, Fort McArthur, Argentia Naval Air Base; there are Canadians, Brits—we'll have the services fight each other."

Dave knew a serviceman's allegiance to his col-

Boxing took servicemen's minds off the war which, as Dave saw first-hand when his ship encountered a U-boat, was never far from the Newfoundland shore. The friendships Dave (back row, second from right) made with other boxers lasted long after the war. Back row, far right: Jimmy Pearson. Front row, far left: Jimmy James; far right: Manny Botaglio. DAVE BROWN COLLECTION

leagues was depthless. Once, in a St. John's dance hall fracas, his buddies had stripped a navy cop off Dave's back. "He was going to arrest me," he recalls. "They said, 'Bullshit!'" A night in a military brig couldn't deter such behaviour. The strength of their feelings for each other was stronger than regulations. Dave also knew of the tensions that existed in wartime Newfoundland, which at the time was not yet a province of Canada. He describes these as a kind of sociological burgoo: Newfoundlanders and Canadians resented British elitism. British servicemen and Newfoundlanders resented Canadian wages. Unmarried young Newfoundland women seemed to prefer British servicemen to Newfoundlanders, and Canadians over the British. When Canadian servicewomen arrived on the island Canadian servicemen abandoned their Newfoundland dates and sought them instead. These observations were anecdotal but widely held as fact.

Some of the strongest emotions were reserved for Americans. In 1942 Americans arrived in St. John's—not in increments, like the Canadians, but en masse. It's more than symbolic that the first large contingent disembarked at St. John's harbour from a converted cruise ship. Four thousand US servicemen marched down the gangplank into St. John's and took over parts of the island. Each of them was a handsome midwesterner with a seven-cent pack of Camels in his pocket and sparkle in his eye. American military projects made the previous efforts look piddling. On Quidi Vidi Street in St. John's, on the shores of Quidi Vidi Lake, they erected a huge base. With little regard for the French in Canada, it was named Fort Pepperell, for William Pepperell, the New England

commander who in 1745 captured the French fortress at
Louisbourg. On the island's south shore, two villages
stood in the way of American strategic interests.
Argentia and Marquise vanished under bulldozers. The
remains of 625 locals were scooped from the local ceme-
tery and moved elsewhere. The Americans built one of
the biggest docks in North America, raised the flag and
declared local rules invalid. When entering a US military
base, drivers switched from the left to right side of the
road. Americans rejected recycled BBC radio broadcasts,
installed their own radio station and played Glenn Miller
instead. Many local establishments did not meet the US
military standards. A memorandum issued to all personnel declared sixteen St. John's cafes and thirteen beer
shops off limits. Booze served at the latter, the note
warned, was so bad as to "frequently" produce "tempo-
rary insanity." This was the sort of advertising no amount
of American dollars could buy, of course, but the locals
felt the insult deeply.

They were loved, they were hated. But the
Americans, like their British and Canadian counterparts,
inspired the kind of feelings that young men often express
in the form of a fist. Before Dave came along, these forces
tended to find outlet in the pubs along Water Street where
Americans and Canadians drank. All Dave did was give
formal expression to the prevailing mood.

When Dave took over the boxing program,
Canadians had not won a card in two years. It was
expected that a man could serve at sea, then come ashore
and fight against boxers who were trained at a well-
equipped base. On one occasion Dave had been at sea for

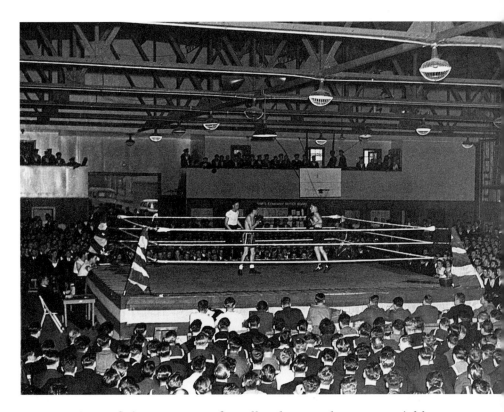

Intraservices fights at Newfoundland's Buckmaster Field gymnasium proved hugely popular with civilians and military personnel. It was Dave's idea to pit Canadian servicemen against their American and British counterparts. ROYAL CANADIAN NAVY PHOTO 2411

six days and was sick most of the time. The second night ashore he was pitted against the US Army's featherweight champion, a tendon-and-muscle slugger also named Brown. The US-made Brown, as the newspapers said, "made a chump of Dave for two rounds." Dave finally got his feet in the third round and hit his opponent through the ropes and into the front row. "It was the only punch I landed," he says, "and a good thing, because I only had one punch in me."

Dave's first order of business as a boxing instructor was to request copies of navy crew lists. He scanned the names for boxers, then, via McCormick's influence, had the men transferred ashore. A systematic exercise program followed. His recruits ran and sparred. They watched their diet. They were navy men, but they were Dave Brown's boxers.

In the next two years Dave staged eleven shows between Canadians and their British and American counterparts. Canadians won eight. In one fight card with US Army and US navy boxers, Canadian fighters won six, drew three and lost one. The fights were wide-open and unpredictable. Among the entrants were Olympic Games contenders and Golden Glove champions. Others were anxious young men eager for recognition. The resulting matches were crowd pleasers. Powerfully built men from Stellarton, Nova Scotia, and Lady Lake, Saskatchewan battled with boxers from rural Kansas and Missouri. Tough guys from Toronto's Cabbage Town were matched with fighters from South Brooklyn. A fight might last forty seconds, others continued after the final bell. The night before a fight, when the mess was serving corned beef hash, Dave and the other fighters feasted on plate-sized steak. The fights played to the divisions in the services. "I had everyone talking boxing," he recalls. Aubrey Mack, a local radio station host, had Dave on air so often people thought he was a broadcaster. When the regular writer for the *Avalon News* couldn't file a story, Dave tapped out accounts for him. Purple as a bruise, Dave's prose shamelessly promoted the fights as the best entertainment in wartime Newfoundland. The fight cards drew audiences of four thousand and more. Only the fire marshals kept the crowds from increasing. The fights were so jammed that the boxers had to battle their way to the ring. When McCormick was made a lieutenant commander, it was said that it was Dave Brown's work as fight organizer that got him the promotion. Stretch a little further and it is possible to make a beer table argument that Dave's work helped convince Newfoundland to join Canada. Newfoundlanders resented American largesse, but in the post-war years when they were choosing their future, many residents argued for the benefits of joining the US. It was the force of the Canadian connection—established during the war and including Dave's boxing cards—that convinced Newfoundlanders their future was in Confederation.

Dave's job had smaller benefits, too. A regular visitor to US bases, he bought army singlets for seventy-five cents apiece and back in Avalon sold them for a dollar. At the time a Canadian serviceman wanting a photo print had to pay twenty-five cents—but it took two months and an act of Parliament to get it. By that time the customer was often transferred, or face down in the North Atlantic. For a dollar, US Army labs delivered a print in two days. Dave developed a brisk middleman business selling prints for two dollars. The scheme was eventually halted when it came to the attention of the admiral. Dave was summoned into headquarters for what may be the shortest disciplinary meeting in military history:

Admiral: "Davey, quit selling those goddamned pictures, will you?"

Dave Brown: "OK, sir. Thank you."

Dave struck up an especially strong friendship with a counterpart in the US Army. With handsomely swept-back hair and a Hollywood chin, Gerry Juracy embodied American bluster. He would phone and say, "Davey, let's have lunch." Before Dave could say he was busy, Juracy cut him off. "Never mind the shit," boomed the voice over the phone. "A car is on its way." "We were buddies," recalls Dave. "We loved each other." At Argentia Dave befriended Tommy Murphy, a quick-talking Detroit native who had fought in a title bout for the world bantamweight championship. Dave knew everyone, and everyone knew him. As a seaman on the *Q078* he was a small part of something big; as a boxing instructor he was a big part of something small.

It was Dave's happiest time of the war. He was boxing regularly. The fights were staged in front of big, roaring audiences. Win or lose, the boxers always got a good round of applause. For days after a fight fellow servicemen would slap Dave on the back and say, "Good job." It was a long way from the brassy elitism of the *Sarcasia*. Even when he lost a fight, which wasn't often, Dave felt good. A photo from the era shows Dave after a loss, at Avalon, surrounded by Royal Canadian Navy and US navy boxers: thirteen rugged, broad-nosed faces and in the middle Dave, white T-shirt over his muscular frame, eyes swollen like ripe purple plums. He's laughing, like someone just told a great joke.

In 1945, a week before his last-ever boxing match, Dave Brown was training in an echoing gymnasium when a clowning heavyweight wrestler grabbed his right shoulder and swung hard. There was a sound like a chicken wing being torn from a carcass and Dave collapsed. When the pain subsided, he worked the arm loose but something was wrong. In the cold night air his shoulder ached. The next week he stepped into the ring at the Argentia Naval Air Base. Dave was fighting as a lightweight—135 pounds; his opponent was a little bigger. Dave figured his shoulder was better but it wasn't. His right hand—the knockout hand—was a pillow full of goosedown. "I took a shit-kicking," he recalls. He laid off training, and his weight ballooned. He never boxed again.

Just before war's end the Halifax fire department asked Dave to stage a fight. Dave contacted Harvey Dubbs, a journeyman fighter who had once shown well against the legendary Sugar Ray Robinson. Then he arranged for Russ Leighton to send a fighter with a bad chin. Leighton dispatched one Carl Brisson, a respectable boxer who could be counted on to go a few rounds before obligingly collapsing. Brisson had a body that sculptors could use for a model, but he lacked durability. Meanwhile, a colleague named Bruce Richardson, who would eventually teach boxing to Hollywood stars, reserved the Halifax arena. On the afternoon of the fight Dave, Dubbs and Richardson were waiting for a taxi on

Sackville Street when, in Dave's word, "boof!" The ground shook and buildings quivered. Glass shards appeared on Dave's shoulder. A mushroom cloud billowed from the harbour. A woman nearby made a sign of the cross. "Oh my god," she wept, "the Germans have got the V2 rocket."

Actually, a munitions depot had caught fire, setting off a series of explosions.

Dave and his companions eventually made their way through the rubble and confusion to the arena. Despite the emergency, a huge crowd was gathered. Just as Dave was climbing into the ring a fire department official told him the event had to be cancelled. The crowd sensed that something was up and they didn't like it. If they couldn't see a fight, they wanted to be in one. Dave had survived submarines and deep seas, but nothing was so threatening as a fight crowd denied. "Ladies and gentlemen," said Dave, "on account of unforeseen circumstances we'll have to cancel the fight until tomorrow." The crowd booed and hollered and moved forward angrily. Serendipitously, just as they reached the ring—boof!—there was another big explosion, the first of a series, and the crowd scrambled for the exits.

Relieved, Brown retreated with Richardson and Dubbs to a Barrington Street Hotel. The hotel had already been damaged and with every ensuing explosion more plaster flaked ominously from the ceiling. Richardson was for doing as the authorities suggested: sleeping in the park. But Dave, survivor of the *U-518*, now an ex-boxer, would have none of it. "Bullshit," he announced. "If we're going to get it, let's get it in bed."

Chapter Five

Dave and Phyllis were married in Verdun's Chalmers United Church on July 21, 1945. A week later they boarded a west-bound train. There was never any doubt in Dave's mind that he wanted to settle in Vancouver; despite living in Scotland and Montreal, he still considered the West Coast home. When Phyllis agreed the issue was resolved. With few savings, they rented a bungalow at 1358 East 2nd Avenue, a half-block off Clark Drive. It was an unassuming structure, with four rooms, a cranky coal furnace, and a big bathtub oddly perched atop stilt-like legs. They lived there for seven years.

Two of the Brown's four daughters, Sandy and Heather, were born while they lived at the 2nd Avenue home. Nine years later Vicki and Lori, separated by three years, completed the family. When Vicki and Lori were young it seemed as if their siblings were more like mothers—

young women concerned with housework and child care. As the girls grew the age differences diminished. Dave, who called his daughters by birth order—#1, #2 . . . —was the pushover parent. Phyllis was not to be crossed. If, for example, she denied a daughter's request for extra pocket money there were no second questions. Dave was hopelessly pliable. "If you wanted something, some money, you'd say, 'Daaaad?'" recalls Lori. "He couldn't say 'No.' He wore his emotions on his sleeve." A family story from Heather and Sandy's childhood centres around the time the girls were blamed for breaking a piece of household furniture. Phyllis determined that Dave should mete out the punishment. He marched the girls into a back room, shut the door, and began whumping a chair. "Dad pretended to spank us and had us howling," recalls Heather.

It was only when the girls were in their teens and started dating that Dave became strict. He was ferociously protective. According to his daughters, he disliked all the boys that they introduced, regardless of how polite or well-groomed they were. "There wasn't one we dated that he didn't try to scare off," recalls Lori. Dave would intercept them at the front door, often clad in underwear, his boxer's face twisted into a nasty snarl, and then tell them to get lost, or else. A young man who showed up at the Browns' front door explained to Dave that he wanted to show off his new car to one of Dave's daughters. "Get in your new car and piss off," was Dave's response. For some young men, the thought of facing the Brown girls' "boxing dad" was too daunting. Sandy semi-secretly dated Brian Kask for months before Brian decided the situation had to change. The son of a local family involved in a successful ready-mix concrete business, with a part-time job as manager of a local lumberyard, he didn't feel he had anything to hide from Dave. When Phyllis saw Brian striding up the drive, she anticipated such a father-suitor blow-up that she scampered into a neighbour's yard. But the explosion never happened. After their talk Dave realized that Brian was a reasonable young man, and from then on treated him well. "He liked me, but he had a funny way of showing it," laughs Brian.

All four girls grew up in a home fanatically devoted to sports. Both parents logged many, many hours driving their children to and from lacrosse, track and field, ice skating and swim competitions. The canopy-covered back of Dave's pickup was like a bus for several school teams. The pre-dawn journey to the Canada Games Pool, where Vicki swam weekdays at 6 a.m. with the Hyack Swim Club, was as much a routine as turning out the lights. Dave was never too tired after work to refuse a game of baseball or football. When Lori, the self-described tomboy of the family, got a notion that she'd like to play school rugby—something unheard of in the early 1970s—it sent her school into a gender-issue tizzy that went all the way to the school board. But Dave and Phyllis backed her fully: if their daughter wanted to play rugby they would stand behind her. Another time Vicki was raising money for her swim club by signing up sponsors for a swimathon. Dave took a sheath of pledge sheets to work—he was with BC Tel—and hit up every employee. Although only nine years old, Vicki completed one hundred lengths and Dave collected a small fortune. When Phyllis was busy, Dave would take one of the girls to the boxing club that he operated in the late 1940s and into the 1950s. All four daughters have scrapbook memories of big, sweaty fighters and stinky gymnasiums. Sandy and Heather, especially, were conscripted by their father to run the round clock, or take statistics in boxing tournaments. And on those nights when the family wasn't actually participating in a sport, Dave transformed their home into a multimedia centre, a Montreal Canadiens game playing on the television in the living room, a baseball broadcast on a set in the den, and another sport blaring from the kitchen radio. "Our friends thought our home was a crazy place," says Sandy. "It was noisy. You could be halfway down the street and know when someone scored a goal."

Around the dinner table, too, talk was often of sport. Dave seems to have been born talking: he is good at it; he talks a lot; and he is completely engrossed while talking. From his seat at the head of the family table, he would pick up the salt shaker, upend it over his dinner and start in with the latest news on the local fight game. If he forgot what his hand was doing, as was often the case, he'd spread so much salt on his dinner that it looked as though it was lightly frosted. As long as he kept talking he never noticed the taste, either. Once, in the interest of experimentation, the family taped the salt shaker closed. Dave sprinkled liberally, as usual, then set in for his meal. Afterwards the incredulous family asked if he'd noticed anything unusual. His response: delicious, as always. Decades later the family still recalled the time Dave obliviously talked and sipped his way through an accidental brew of tea and coffee.

What the daughters came to realize—as they grew and met friends' fathers—is that Dave was both unusually energetic and unusually emotional. The slightest mishap would set him off. The crisis of erecting the canvas tent on the family's annual Okanagan camping trip was always good for a frenzied session of anger and profanity. While the girls were off horse riding on one of these camping trips, Dave and Phyllis decided to take a walk and made a wrong turn. They came back slightly late, with Dave in the midst of a full-blown conniption—his girls! Alone! They were fine, of course, flopped in the family car sipping soft drinks.

In later years, when his daughters were married and starting families of their own, Dave's emotions intensified. Vicki recalls being pregnant and going to the hospital with her father for routine tests. When one test indicated a potential problem—but not a crisis—Dave ran for the phone. "He was crying to Mom, 'Something's wrong, something's wrong,'" she says. Later, after delivering a healthy baby girl, Vicki phoned her parents with the good news. Dave held on to the receiver only long enough to hear that everything was fine. "Then he dropped the phone and started crying," says Vicki. "He was convinced one of us wasn't going to make it."

A former boxer with navy skills in signals did not have the job choices that an electrical engineer or a welder had in post-war Vancouver, but that never bothered Dave. In his mind, a good, hard-working blue-collar worker deserves no more or less respect than a good, hard-working professional. After a brief stint repairing municipal bridges, he took a job slinging beer in the Metropolitan Hotel. That lasted until a female patron goosed him as he was passing with a tray and he lost control of two dozen glasses of draft. A position with the liquor distribution branch didn't work out, either. Hired for the Christmas rush, Dave was offered a full-time job on condition that he join the Liberal party. He might as well have been asked to wear a kimono.

When word went out that the Canadian Imperial Bank of Commerce was looking for couriers, Dave applied. His security check consisted of the bank manager giving him a good looking over. Dave appeared to be straight so the manager gave him a pistol and a bag of money and said, "Go." On foot, or in a cab, Dave chauffeured hundreds of thousands of dollars between the bank's downtown branches. Some people might have felt a certain tension carrying that kind of money, but not Dave. He liked the freedom of the job; once out of range of the ever-testy managers he could do as he pleased. He pocketed his taxi money and walked across town, a fortune in bills tucked under his arm. Once, while ferrying one hundred $1,000 bills from the Bank of Canada on Pender Street to the Bank of Commerce at Hastings and Granville, he spotted a theatre that was playing a movie that he wanted to see, so he ducked in. When he walked into the bank several hours later, the anxious manager said, "They're all wondering where the hell you are." Dave tossed money on the desk. "Piss on it, you got your money. Quit worrying."

In 1948 Dave took a job in the stores department of Canadian Telephone and Supply, the precursor to BC Tel and Telus. He stayed for thirty-five years.

To lace on gloves and willingly step into a ring with another boxer requires such a level of courage that to rank fighters by victory only is to ignore their greatest triumph: being there. Boxing differs from other sports. As Joyce Carol Oates writes, you can play baseball, or football or hockey. No one plays boxing.

The game evolves around central fighters. Muhammad Ali is one, of course. So was Jack Johnson. And Joe Louis. And the Sugar Rays—Leonard and Robinson. More than dominant characters, though they were that, too, their style in and out of the ring transformed their names into symbols for dominance, dignity, innovation, relentlessness.

Vancouver's Jimmy McLarnin was such a boxer. Twice holder of the world welterweight title, an electrifying puncher who took on the toughest fighters in a tough era, McLarnin is the pivot on which West Coast boxing swings. His story intersects and orders BC fighting—the bare-knuckle frontier duke-outs, the showboat exhibitions, the hard-hearted smokers—and everyone involved in the fight game: the Billy Townsends, the Tommy Paonessas, the Dave Browns.

James McLarnin was born in Belfast in 1907, but as a youngster moved to Canada with his family and was raised in Vancouver's east end. His father, Sam, was an elastic immigrant, snapping from Ireland to the Alberta foothills, back to Ireland and then, as a married man, to a Manitoba farm and finally west to Vancouver, where he ran a second-hand-furniture store and raised a family in the years after World War I. Sam and his wife had twelve children. Jimmy was the second-oldest.

"Our street was Union Street, not far from the docks in Vancouver," McLarnin recalled in *Maclean's* in 1950. "Some people would call it a poor street, and some people would call it a tough street, but to me it was a good street because there was always something going on." For his tenth birthday Jimmy McLarnin received two pairs of boxing gloves and, holding them aloft prophetically, vowed to become champion. He laced the gloves on and then set off down the street, swinging his arms menacingly. The first boy he met he clocked. Jimmy McLarnin was 1–0. Along the street came another boy. He clocked Jimmy. One for two, Jimmy stumbled home and hung the gloves on a nail, vowing to work on his soccer skills. Had it not been for a family friend, that would have been it for Jimmy McLarnin's fight career.

Charles Foster was a sturdy middle-aged longshoreman with wire-brush hair, enormous hands and a broad nose that spoke to a long and highly personal involvement in boxing. "Pop," as he was known, was born into an English fighting family that celebrated a boy's first jab instead of his first step. As a teenager, Pop was a booth fighter in an uncle's boxing circus, a kind of fistic travelling carnival. Pop took on all comers, regardless of size, with bare knuckles or gloves. For every round a challenger survived, Pop's father paid

Two-time world welterweight champion Jimmy McLarnin grew up on Vancouver's tough Union Street and his successes sparked a 1930s renaissance in Vancouver boxing. Although he retired in the US he returned often to visit family and help with sport fundraisers.
CITY OF VANCOUVER ARCHIVES CVA 553-E-2

one pound. He took on as many as fifteen challengers a day and if he didn't kayo at least a dozen of them in a round or less he didn't eat.

Though service in the Boer War and World War I took Pop away from professional boxing and left him with a permanent limp, he was aware of large-scale changes that were transforming the sport. The most significant of these was the adoption of Marquis of Queensberry Rules over the long-standing London Prize Ring Rules. At one time derided for making sissies out of fighters, the London Prize Rules were formulated by an eighteenth-century butcher-cum-boxer named Jack Broughton and banned such early fight tactics as kneeing, kicking, biting and—especially common and effective—hitting in the crotch. Broughton's regulations stipulated that fights be segmented into rounds and between rounds fighters could rest for thirty seconds. He also made fighters wear gloves—not to reduce head injuries, as is widely believed, but to prevent damage to boxers' hands.

Broughton's suggestions were so successful they became the standard in boxing for more than a century and in some cases have permanently entered the English language. According to Broughton's rules: fighters were not allowed to "hit below the belt"; before each round they had to "come to scratch"—a line in the turf—also known as "toeing the line"; when the men in a boxer's corner saw that their man was beaten, they "threw in the towel."

By the late 1800s, public concern over the bloody nature of prizefighting—and the kind of bloody, bare-knuckle shows Pop was involved in—forced reform upon the sport. Adopted in 1889, the Queensberry Rules declared:

> 1. To be a fair stand-up boxing match, in a twenty-four foot ring, or as near that size as practicable.
> 2. No wrestling or hugging allowed.
> 3. The rounds to be of three minutes' duration, and one minute's time between rounds.
> 4. If either man fall through weakness or otherwise, he must get up unassisted, ten seconds to be allowed him to do so, the other man meanwhile to return to his corner, and when the fallen man is on his legs the round is to be resumed, and continued until the three minutes have expired. If one man fails to come to scratch in the ten seconds allowed, it shall be in the power of the referee to give his award in favour of the other man.
> 5. A man hanging on the ropes in a helpless state, with his toes off the ground, shall be considered down.
> 6. No seconds or any other person to be allowed in the ring during the rounds.
> 7. Should the contest be stopped by any unavoidable interference, the referee to name the time and place as soon as possible for finishing the contest; so that the match must be won and lost, unless the

backers of both men agree to draw the
stakes.

8. The gloves to be fair-sized boxing
gloves of the best quality, and new.

9. Should a glove burst, or come off, it
must be replaced to the referee's satisfaction.

10. A man on one knee is considered
down, and if struck is entitled to the stakes.

11. No shoes or boots with springs
allowed.

12. The contest in all other respects to
be governed by the revised rules of the
London Prize Ring.

The Queensberry Rules, as they came to be called, were
more a reaction to forces outside boxing than they were
to anything within the sport. In the late 1800s, a number
of forces converged to try to prohibit boxing. Most powerful of these were the anti-prizefighting leagues in
England and North America. Sisters to the Prohibition
movements of the day, they declared that the blood, violence and graft generic to prizefighting were antithetical
to the values of the modern "progressive" era. The twen-
tieth century was going to be an era of high civilization—
of music and books and philosophy—and the flesh and
blood of fighting needed to be consigned, like square-
riggers and slavery, to history. Even after widespread
acceptance of the Queensberry Rules, which many of
boxing's traditionalists thought made far too many concessions, calls for the abolition of the sport continued

until World War I. Then, suddenly, pacifism was out and violence was fashionable. Boxing, with its soldier-like creeds of discipline and personal sacrifice, was once again regarded as virtuous. By war's end, boxing was among the most popular sports in England and North America.

To succeed in this new era, Pop knew, a boxer would require technique as well as natural strength. In young Jimmy McLarnin—in the unusual stockiness of his legs, in his agility—Pop saw the makings of a superb athlete. He made Sam McLarnin an offer: give him the boy, and he'd deliver a champion.

He looked like an old country tradesman, but there was a lot of science behind Pop's casual, tweed-and-pipe-smoke exterior. One of the first things he did was force the right-handed McLarnin to live left-handed. The boy threw darts left-handed, he swung the axe left-handed. In a space cleared in the cluttered basement of his Sam's second-hand store, Pop put McLarnin through nightly exercises, skipping and shadow boxing. When the boy was in shape, Pop worked on his balance. Recalled McLarnin, "Pop made me shadow box and punch the bag with a book balanced on top of my head and I began to learn how to move around quickly and still avoid the abrupt and jerky head movements that can make you lose sight momentarily and sometimes disastrously of an opponent's eyes or hands." To build the boy's neck muscles, Pop salvaged a twelve-pound weight from a butcher's scales and tied two leather thongs to it. Then he sat McLarnin on the edge of a chair, put the thongs in his teeth and made him swing the weight back and forth.

Afterwards the boy tumbled into bed feeling like someone had tried to rip his jaw off.

The McLarnins could not afford the best fare for a young boxer—steaks, lamb chops, fresh fruit and vegetables—so to compensate for his less-than-ideal diet, McLarnin forswore candy and ice cream. When the neighbourhood kids were working up a baseball game, he was doing roadwork. When friends went swimming at the seashore, he punched the bag in the dingy basement. He skipped rope until his legs were numb, studied the jab, did an honours degree in defence. "Getting hit doesn't teach you not to get hit," he said years later, virtually quoting Pop. "Getting hit too often slows down your reflexes. The more you get hit, the easier you become to hit, and the easier you become to hit, the more often you get hit."

What Pop was doing was training McLarnin to be a boxer, not a fighter. Fighters were artless sluggers, tough guys who favoured bicep size over technique. Sometimes they fought in a ring, frequently not. British Columbia's history brims with accounts of such battles. Two Natives hammered each other on Victoria's Johnston Street and the *British Colonist* reported it as a legitimate sporting event, a "spirited bout" that exhibited "considerable science." Sometimes all it took to make a fight legitimate in turn-of-the-century BC was a roof. In 1907 James Barnswell, a sealer, fought Oliver Fisher, a bartender, in a Goldstream stable. The fight ended when Fisher delivered a punch so hard it lifted Barnswell the height of an apple crate off the floor. One of the meanest of the province's early fighters was George Wilson, who trained on rum and was stoop-shouldered, hairless, bowlegged and cross-eyed.

Many pre-Queensberry Rules fights were longer than they were good. Twenty- and thirty-round bouts were commonplace. In 1866, two BC boxers participated in one of the longest matches in Canadian prizefighting history. Joe Eden and George Baker fought for the championship of Vancouver Island on a rocky shelf on the shores of Pedder Bay, near Victoria. Eden, twenty-seven, was British-born and said to have a head as hard as a ram's. Baker, thirty-three, was a quick-handed Canadian. The chronicles of the actual fight are slim and no wonder. A thorough account would have filled a full-edition broadsheet. A reporter trying to cover each round would have worn out a pocketful of hard-leaded pencils. As it was, the fight's chroniclers were forced into a pugilistic shorthand: round 5: Baker down "with some violence"; rounds 6–12: "about even"; round 13: Eden down; round 23: ditto; by the fortieth round there were "heavy exchanges"; round 63: both men visibly tiring; rounds 119 and 120: Baker staggering up to scratch, only to be slammed down by Eden's wicked right. Finally, in round 128, and one hour and fifty minutes after the match had begun, Eden dropped Baker with a hard right hook. Following tradition, he vaulted the ropes to claim his purse.

By the time Jimmy McLarnin was sixteen he had fought and won a dozen local amateur matches and Pop was convinced they were ready for the rich American professional scene. McLarnin was superbly balanced, graceful, disciplined, tough and durable. At the time the two boarded a San Francisco-bound steamer, McLarnin stood 4'10" and weighed 108 pounds.

When McLarnin won his first professional fight, a

Part of boxing's appeal has always been simplicity. These boxers are sparring on a wooden platform erected on the receding edge of Vancouver's forest, circa 1912. CITY OF VANCOUVER ARCHIVES CVA7-181

four-round preliminary in Oakland over Frankie Sands, no one paid much attention. But then he won his next ten fights and the crusty San Francisco press took note. When "Baby Face," as he was known, had beaten the area's best fighters, he and Pop worked their way to Los Angeles on a tramp steamer. The city's fight scene was a step up from San Francisco's, but McLarnin did well. He beat Fidel La Barba, winner of the flyweight gold medal at the 1924 Olympics. He lost a close fight to Bud Taylor, then won a startlingly easy ten-round, non-title fight over Pancho Villa, the former flyweight world champion. "After the Villa fight," McLarnin recalled, "the things that happen in books started happening to me." He beat Mickey Gill and Jackie Fields, a former Olympic gold medallist, in Los Angeles. Then he developed jaundice, lost weight, contemplated giving up the sport. For six months he languished, teetering, at age nineteen, on the edge of has-been. Pop convinced him to move east and try again. In Chicago, a promoter set him against Louis "Kid" Kaplan, a former featherweight champion who was dominating the Midwest. The prevailing thinking in the city was that McLarnin was going to be an easy knock-down.

All the gamblers with money on Kaplan liked what happened in the first round. The bell rang and McLarnin strode into a left hook that broke his jaw and knocked him flat. He beat the count, but was unsteady. He was knocked down in the second, mauled in the third. His defensive style wasn't working. Between rounds Pop bent to the battered boy's ear and suggested a change in tactics. "Jimmy, why don't *you* try hitting *him*." At the bell McLarnin rose from his seat, stumbled unsurely into the ring, and missed Kaplan with a roundhouse punch. He swung again and again, mostly missing but the offence took Kaplan aback, and in that time McLarnin's head cleared. His punches connected. It was Kaplan's turn to fight on his heels. In the eighth round McLarnin landed two rights to Kaplan's chin. Kaplan's eyes fogged. McLarnin did the math on another right and swung. Kaplan was out before he hit the canvas.

McLarnin was still getting his post-fight rub-down when Pop got a call from Jess McMahon. McMahon was matchmaker for Tex Rickard, the promoter who made Jack Dempsey's career. Rickard controlled the switch that turned fights on or off at Madison Square Garden, the epicentre of North American professional boxing. Would Jimmy be interested in fighting in New York, asked McMahon. Jimmy McLarnin was going big time.

Back in Vancouver, reports of McLarnin's successes did to the local fight scene what a warm May rain does to a freshly seeded field. At church and Scout camps, at schools and colleges, boxing became *the* sport. Amateur bouts were staged outdoors, in parks and public spaces. One observer, riding a tram to Steveston, noted a number of families had set up makeshift rings in their backyards, where dads gave lessons to boys in the hope that they, too, might become little Jimmys. When the weather turned foul, these same hopefuls sought shelter to practise their sport wherever they could, in lofts, garages, even the confines of the Silver Slipper Ballroom. The Number 5 Firehall on Vernon Drive, draughty and as chill as a tunnel, opened its doors in winter to would-be boxers, who jogged and skipped and jabbed alongside the pumper trucks. When the firehall became unbearably cold the same clutch of fighters moved into an empty building on Hastings Street, near Main. It was warmer but lacked lights, so they sparred to the blinking lights of the marquee from the nearby Pantages Theatre. When the lights flashed on, the kids threw punches; when they flashed off, they backed away.

The goal of many of these young men was to fight professionally: to get paid—or at least have the chance of

There was no bigger attraction in Vancouver in the 1930s than a Jimmy McLarnin fight. Before the era of television, and when many people could not afford radios, fans listened to fight broadcasts in stores and restaurants. Here a crowd gathers at the city's Brown Bros. Bakery to listen to McLarnin's 1934 title defence in New York against arch-rival Barney Ross. CITY OF VANCOUVER ARCHIVES CVA99-4418

getting paid—for boxing. In the 1920s, that was the best measure of a boxer's proficiency and a number of clubs staged professional fights: the Beaver Club at Robson and Granville; the Lester Lounge on Cordova Street; the Cedar Cottage at Commercial Avenue and 18th; the Orange Hall at Hastings and Gore. But the centre of Vancouver's

The enthusiasm of Sam and Jimmy McLarouse for boxing was typical of Vancouver in the mid-1920s. Makeshift rings and homemade punching bags dotted backyards and every neighbourhood had at least one fight club. Boxing was thought to teach young men discipline and the value of conditioning. CITY OF VANCOUVER ARCHIVES CVA 99-1575

boxing universe was indisputably the Calvary Club, at Granville and Smythe. Dark-wooded, atmosphere heavy with the smoke of cheap cigars, the Calvary Club offered to young boxers what the Roman Coliseum offered to Christians: a long-shot chance at glory. The fight-savvy crowd could cheer a boxer on one moment, then be booing and catcalling him the next. When the ring action failed to slake the crowd's thirst for mayhem, the stony-faced observers notified the combatants with a chorus from the love song, "Let Me Call You Sweetheart," or derisively called, "Go back to the docks! . . . I got the next dance! . . . Put out the lights, they want to be alone!"

Jack Allen ran boxing at the Calvary Club. Called "Jack" by some, "Deacon" by others, and much worse by many more, Allen had come to Vancouver in 1918 after his promising career as an Alaskan bootlegger was fore-shortened by the authorities. He set about organizing fights and hired George Paris as his trainer. Paris, a black Nova Scotian, was working in Vancouver when Jack Johnson arrived for his bout with Victor McLaglen in 1909. In Paris, Johnson discovered one of the few men capable of keeping up with and possibly surpassing him. But Paris never got that chance. A black-on-black prize-fight wouldn't have drawn the kind of money Johnson demanded. Instead, Paris remained Johnson's sparring partner for half a decade. When Paris returned to Vancouver in the 1920s he joined forces with Allen: Allen did the paperwork; Paris ran the gym. The two produced some good fighters: tough guy Vic Foley, talented Angelo Branca (who went on to become a Supreme Court justice) and Vancouver's greatest could-have-been, Billy Townsend.

Billy Townsend's story resembles Jimmy McLarnin's story, minus the mindful tutelage of Pop Foster. Like McLarnin he was the sports-keen son of an immigrant. In 1907, when Billy was two, his father came from Durham, England, to work in the Nanaimo coal mines. When Billy was twelve, he, too, went into collieries. In his off-hours he fought amateur bouts for Nanaimo's Hopes and Has Beens Club. He liked to fight, and he was good. Work in the mines had given him a powerful upper body and great endurance. When he saw in a newspaper ad "Wanted: Men to fight, 15 to 60" he knew it had been posted for him. Still a teenager, he caught a steamer to Vancouver and, ad in hand, marched into the Calvary Club. Allen, unlike Pop Foster, was keen to get newcomers fighting right away. Paris did what he could to prep Townsend but he only had hours, not years. The first Saturday Townsend was in Vancouver, he kayoed a boy from Victoria. By Wednesday he was in a Bellingham ring where he flattened an opponent in round one. Liking what he saw in the burly coal miner, Allen signed Townsend to a contract.

When Townsend had wiped out the local competition, Allen took him to Los Angeles in 1930 to fight Amador Santiago, a relentless puncher and tough as canvas. In the first six rounds, Santiago had Townsend on the mat six times. In the seventh round, Santiago sent Townsend to the mat again. Townsend recalled what happened next: "I got up at the count of nine, all blurred, and all I could see was a big black shadow—man, he was black—comin' at me. I swung a right hand and caught him under the heart and at the same time he tagged me right on the chin." Both boxers went down—a clean double knockout.

The bell ending the round had gone before the boxers were flattened so they were both technically still in the fight. In the corners the crews struggled to revive their charges. Townsend's second corner man was "Jerry the

Greek," who had trained Jack Dempsey. He slapped Townsend around, sloshed water over his head, all to no avail. With just moments remaining before round eight was to begin, Jerry the Greek lit a match under Townsend's spine: "He shoved me out in the ring at the bell. I was still out on my feet so I grabbed the ropes and hung on. I heard the referee counting but I didn't know what was going on. It wasn't until the next day that I found out that I'd won by a knockout. Amador couldn't come out of his corner and the referee had counted him out."

In a rematch, Townsend kayoed Santiago in seven. He was on his way—or so he thought. But Deacon Allen was more interested in setting up fighters than he was in fighting set-ups. After Billy Townsend's win over Santiago, the two travelled to New York. With Allen accepting any and all comers, Townsend beat Eddie Ryan, Paulie Walker and Andy Saviola. They were good fighters, but the matches lacked the kind of attraction they would have had if Townsend had more of a history. And without a reputation he couldn't afford a poor showing. After a lot of wrangling, Allen managed to get Townsend a fight with top-ranked Billie Petrolle. Petrolle destroyed Townsend in seven rounds. That loss might have been forgivable, but then Allen scheduled a quick rematch with Eddie Ryan. Townsend, unprepared, was knocked out in the second round. Two quick victories and he lost successively to Joey Goodman, Benny Leonard, Battling Battilo and Freddie Steele. With his fighter's stock cellar-bound, Allen arranged a title fight with the resilient Tony Canzoneri. When Townsend's head struck the canvas his career was over. With few savings, he married and took a job driving a dump truck for the City of Vancouver. In 1936, he attempted a comeback. He won twelve fights, then was knocked out in the thirteenth round of the thirteenth bout. He never fought again.

The difference between a Pop Foster and a Deacon Allen is the difference between a gardener and a fast-food customer: one nurtures, toils, then reaps; the other has a bite en route to something else. One has patience; the other does not.

In New York, Pop Foster studied the rosters of other managers, looking for a boxer who would give Jimmy McLarnin a good, entertaining fight, but who would not likely win. He found such a match in Sid Terris. "The Ghost of the Ghetto," as Terris was known, was well-regarded but lacked the ability to finish fighters. He was quick and a good puncher but, thought Pop, not as quick or good as McLarnin. Terris was Jewish, and the matchup with an Irishman had the added advantage of playing to two big constituencies in New York. Although a Protestant and from Belfast, McLarnin was hyped as "the Murderous Mick" and "Dublin Dynamite." Twenty thousand fight fans watched the newcomer knock the familiar Terris out at 1:47 of the first round. For that fight McLarnin and Pop collected $19,000.

Said McLarnin, "For nine years I went—as the saying goes among old fighters and actors—big in New York." McLarnin was invited to a reception by New York mayor

Jimmy Walker. He played golf with Fred Astaire, chummed with Bing Crosby, was photographed with Jean Harlow. Wherever he went people liked him. He was kind, generous, moderate. "I never had to be told that wine, women and song would ruin a boxer," he said. "It had been drummed into me that wine, women and song could ruin *any*body."

McLarnin fought eleven past and present champions before finally taking the title. He battled Sammy Mandell, Ruby Goldstein, Al Singer, the aging Benny Leonard. For every fight he won he moved up two notches on the scale of respectability. For every fight he lost, he moved down one. He did not win each fight, but he didn't need to, thanks to Pop's assiduous management.

McLarnin retired in November, 1935, one month short of his twenty-ninth birthday. He had $500,000. His wits were acute, but he had lost his will to fight and wanted to play golf and start a family with his childhood sweetheart from Vancouver. He quit and never came back—a most unusual ending. His success had inspired a generation of Vancouver boxers and he was satisfied, even if Pop wasn't. "There's just one thing I'm sorry about, Jim," Pop said to McLarnin many years later. "Your left hand—it never did get as good as it should."

Dave Brown likes to tell a story about fighting Jimmy McLarnin. Actually, it's a story about a fight his mother had with McLarnin, but it goes like this: "One day when I was little I was playing in front of our house on Napier Street. And Jimmy McLarnin comes along. He was pretty well known then. He did a lot of his roadwork on a grassy area we called The Flats. So he started boxing with me. I guess he got a bit rough and made me cry. My mother was always watching out. She says, 'What are you doin' to me laddie?' McLarnin says, 'I was only playin'. I didn't mean to hurt him.' But my mother drove him off. When my father got home from work and heard what she had done he said, 'Are you crazy? Do you know who that is?' And she said, 'I'll not have anyone making my Davey cry.'"

In the 1940s and '50s, when Dave was coaching a group of remarkable young Lower Mainland boxers, he'd tell this story by way of introducing them to Pop Foster. Foster, up for a visit from his home in California, would fold his liverspotted hands over his cane and recount his career and explain how he trained McLarnin. Coming from the coach of a former champion who knew all the big names of boxing, it helped them refocus their efforts. The sum of Pop's message was: listen to the coach.

Dave got into coaching soon after he and Phyllis arrived in Vancouver in the summer of 1945. At that time the city's boxing scene was like a top-flight fighter with a bad attitude: it was vibrant, with fight clubs in every neighbourhood, but the overall scene was handicapped by a sort of low-level ineptness in organization, promotion and, especially, training. At the Eagletime Athletic Club, and elsewhere, Dave saw that kids were being pushed beyond their abilities. "A kid would walk in and they'd feel his arm one night, and have him fighting the next night. I said, 'This is horseshit.' You've got to prepare kids." He asked his brother-in-law, Roy Cavallin, a former Vancouver lacrosse star with the Vancouver Burrards (and future trainer with the BC Lions) if he would be interested in helping with a boxing club. When Cavallin said yes, Dave started looking.

The Burrard Athletic Club, as Dave's club was originally known, found its first home in the Irish Fusiliers' Armouries near Stanley Park, but it was inconvenient for east-end kids. So, when word went around that there was space available—the fifth floor, two up from the morgue—in the Vancouver Police Building on Keefer Street, the club moved. As Dave recalls, the floor had been ignored for years, and he and the club's boxers cleaned the place "about thirteen times" before it was usable. Fighting under the name Police Mutual Benevolent Association, or PMBA, the club worked out of Keefer Street for half a decade. When that arrangement ended, the club moved to the basement of the Patricia Hotel on Hastings Street.

Though the name and location would change, the club's central features—Dave, a gang of young men intent on boxing—were the most formidable team in the postwar Vancouver amateur boxing scene, as well as significant players in American and international boxing. Len Walters, Bobby Shires, Len Kupchak, Hughie Meikle, Norm Jorgenson and Buddy Pearson each won a Canadian amateur title once, and several earned titles repeatedly. Brothers Harry and Jackie Schreiber and Normy and Gordy McLeod were outstanding juvenile boxers, as was Jimmy Walters. Dave's fighters consistently won top-level Pacific Northwest competitions, and several made British Empire Games and Olympic appearances. For a decade, "Dave's boys," as they were called, were at the top flight of BC amateur boxing.

From the beginning, Dave emphasized boxing skills over competition. Boxing skills began with physical fitness: exercises to strengthen the neck, stomach and leg muscles, skipping rope, heaving a medicine ball. A visitor to a weekday evening workout at the PMBA gym might witness twelve or fifteen boys in the ring all at once, heaving medicine balls at each other while Dave exhorted them to work ever harder. On weekend mornings he'd criss-cross the city in his sedan rounding up his keenest fighters, then send them off for a run with the promise that if they went flat out he'd spring for a boxer's breakfast on the way home.

Archie McDonald had been boxing for a few years when he started training with Dave. A Vancouver College student, and later a long-time *Vancouver Sun* sports writer, McDonald began boxing under the tutelage of the college's Brother O'Grady. He had participated in several tournaments, and in grade eleven won the 119-pound division in Vancouver's Emerald Gloves competition. Before the brothers made him stop boxing, McDonald worked briefly with Dave, and made a memorable appearance on the Seattle fight program *King's Ring*. As a student at the University of BC, McDonald returned to Dave's club. By this time it had moved from the Keefer Street police station to the basement of the Patricia Hotel on Hastings Street. The club, sponsored by Bill "Blondie" Wallace, owner of Wallace Transfer, and a bootlegger to the police, was called the Wallace AC. The gym, recalls McDonald, was right out of a movie. "That was quite a place. It really was a basement. You slipped in through the beer parlour. There was a ring, and a shower in one

Three of Dave's successful Police Mutual Benevolent Association boxers (l–r): flamboyant Buddy Pearson, journeyman Bobby Shires, technically masterful Len Walters. DAVE BROWN COLLECTION

corner. It was a good atmosphere. Dave always had people down there."

One thing that hadn't changed was Dave's insistence on physical conditioning. McDonald was in excellent shape, but Dave's program was tougher than anything he'd seen. After two months with the Wallace AC he was asked to participate in the mile run as part of UBC's popular intramural games. He didn't consider himself a runner but signed on anyway. McDonald finished second, behind an elite UBC rower.

When a boy was in shape, Dave drilled him in the defensive elementals of boxing. "He taught you how to throw punches and how to avoid punches," recalls McDonald. "You could always tell a Dave Brown–trained boxer. Their left foot was pointed ahead, not sideways. Right hand: tucked under the chin. So it was a short distance to block a shot. And after a clinch, they always touched their hands to their temples. They were ready."

Only when he was able to properly defend himself would a boy be invited to a match. Dave arranged fights in clubs all over the Lower Mainland, or staged matches as entertainment for Rotary Club and Royal Canadian Legion branches. They fought in small halls in the Fraser Valley and Port Moody, and the cavernous Exhibition Gardens. They travelled to Seattle tournaments so often that the waitresses at the Home Cafe in Blaine were shouting orders to the cook before they took their seats. And the sleepy clerk at Seattle's Olympic Hotel didn't have to ask about sleeping arrangements. He knew Dave's boys always slept three to a room. To forestall the boy's pre-fight nerves, Dave carried a deck of cards in his pocket. Whenever there was a hold-up, he'd slap it onto the table and say, "OK. Who's for three-card monte?"

Dave's emphasis on physical conditioning and technique impressed local boxing enthusiasts who were keen to help out. "I seen the way he handled his kids, that the most important thing was the welfare of his kids," says Mario Caravetta, a former corner man for the PMBA. Caravetta, who had a half dozen amateur fights during the war, and later was a trainer with the Western Hockey League's Vancouver Canucks, had seen too many coaches mistreat their young boxers: handlers who withheld meal money when a kid fought poorly; coaches who repeatedly favoured their more successful fighters at the expense of kids who wanted to box for sport, or who were unwilling to accommodate different styles. Dave, says Caravetta, wasn't like that. "He didn't like to cookie-cutter them—he didn't try to develop them into the same-style fighter. He wasn't in the game for what glory he could get for himself. He taught them effort; you're going to get an honest effort from a Dave Brown–trained fighter."

Of the many PMBA boxers Dave Brown coached the most successful and enigmatic was Len Walters. Even when he was on his way to an eventual amateur fight record of 139–10, there was still doubt about his talents. "I don't know if he can take a punch," mused Pop Foster after watching Walters spar. Walters was a technically excellent boxer, though in a confounding way. Some said he was "scientific"; others called him "defensive." *Vancouver Sun* reporter Dick Beddoes said he was "slicker

Two generations of Vancouver boxers in the ring: referee Hector McDonald, a fine lightweight once known as "Phantom," watches as Len Walters sticks it to an opponent. DAVE BROWN COLLECTION

than a thin dime on a wet beer table." *Sun* sports editor Erwin Swangard said Walters had "educated fists" and "educated legs." The only thing anyone knew for sure was that Len Walters won with the regularity of North Shore rain.

Walters was born in 1931 Vancouver to the kind of mildly dysfunctional family that often produces boxers. His father, Charles, a forlorn-looking man with the weight of misfortune on his face, was a sometime carpenter and sometime at-home parent. His mother raised her children in difficult circumstances. As a Vancouver newspaper reporter put it, "Len didn't always have the chance to decision three square meals a day." When Walters was twelve a friend took him to a boxing match. He was hooked.

Walters started boxing for Val Roche, of the Eagletime Athletic Club, one of the clubs where Dave noted young boxers were being prematurely rushed into competition. Besides having what Dave would call a shitty attitude, Eagletime operated from the bottom of the Penthouse Club, a Seymour Street speakeasy associated with everything that could possibly be unwholesome for a young boxer: bootlegging, gambling, all-night drinking and carousing. Except for a footnote in city chronicles as the place where crooner Harry Belafonte knocked out a pestering customer with a punch to the nose, there was nothing about the Penthouse that suggested it was a good place to train impressionable young fighters. Roach hurried Walters, then sixty-five pounds, into his first fight, held at the Vancouver Seamen's Club. He lost to Larry Creanza and wept.

When word went around that newcomer Dave Brown was running a disciplined club, Walters joined. He was a lanky youth, with slicked-back hair, long, lean arms and a toothy grin. As he did with every newcomer, Dave gave Walters a brief introductory lecture. "I said, 'I don't mess around with kids who are wasting my time. If some guy is kibitzing, pissing around, I say, OK. Get dressed. You are *not* wasting my time.'" He showed Walters his attendance sheet. If a kid didn't come for workouts he didn't fight. It was that simple. Walters liked Dave's straightforward style and soon was a club regular, busing over three times a week from King Edward school. He worked hard, had great footwork. After several months in the gym, Dave entered Walters in the city's annual Golden Gloves tournament.

Originally started to promote athletics for working-class kids in the eastern United States, the Golden Gloves were to post-war Vancouver what Earth Day and the Vancouver Marathon were to the city decades later. Sponsored by the *Vancouver Sun* and, later, the *Province*, they were among the biggest sporting events on the city calendar. They drew thousands of fans, and a boxer who showed well was rewarded with something of celebrity status.

Not only did Walters win his first Golden Glove in 1945, but he won convincingly. Then he won the next year, and the next. Within three years of appearing on the city amateur fight scene, Len Walters and Dave Brown were regarded as the best duo in city boxing. In Seattle, where the Golden Gloves were even more popular than in Vancouver, Walters had the lead role in a Brown-coached team that stunned the locals. "Our first impression when we saw these guys from Vancouver: worried," says long-time Washington State amateur coach Dick Francisco. Francisco, a former military pilot, was building up his own remarkable group of boxers in the Greenwood Boys Club, eventual winners of a US national amateur boxing team championship. "We knew we were up against some really good and well-trained fighters. There was no 'yeahs' or 'naws,' little or no profanity. They were well-coached. They looked good." Just how good the Americans discovered when Walters met Greenwood's Dickie Ralls in 1947, in a final that was talked about for years afterwards.

For the first two rounds the coaches let the boxers fight untethered: Ralls, a precocious slugger, tagged Walters with harder punches, but Walters was swifter, and scored with lightning jabs. Between the second and third rounds Dave told Walters to pick up the pace even more, to run his opponent into the ground. Ralls faded in the last minute and the fight was Walters'. In the coming years the two boxers would meet three more times, taking two wins each. "They had some of the best wars you'd ever want to see," says Francisco.

By 1948, while still a teenager, Walters had won three (of an eventual six) Vancouver Golden Glove titles, and the first of four senior BC boxing championships. Fighting as a bantamweight, he captured the Canadian Open Boxing Championship in 1949 and again in 1952.

Determined to dissect Walters' winning style, reporter Dick Beddoes followed him through a workout. Here is what he saw:

> [He] was battling the heavy bag, thudding it with the appetizing smack of a cork yanked from a whisky bottle. The way it was going, it looked bad for the bag. The fighter looked like he'd "win easy."
>
> After ten minutes of abusing the heavy sack, the fighter addressed his attention to the light speed bag, which is a glob of

leather surrounding some air. The speed bag didn't have it any easier. It whacked against the backboard with the kind of rat-tat-tat sound that makes a soldier duck when he hears it coming out of a machine gun. A killing sound. After 11 minutes the speed bag was spent. Came then three brisk rounds of sparring with live punching bags. Working with human targets, the fighter looked the skilled professional practising with ease all the things a boxer should do.

He stuck and moved, jabbed and hooked and bobbed, threw a right cross that was as straight as a line drive whistling over third base. He scored with crisp left jabs, dug deep with both hands to the body, let his spar-mates work him against the ropes and then slipped away like fog.

To Walters' natural ability Dave added his knowledge of boxing, the techniques and strategy. "I would think that he was always right on everything," Walters wryly recalls. "OK; maybe that's confidence. Maybe it's over-confidence. He would never give up on anything that he thought he was right about. Dave has a mind of his own. What he thinks is right is supposed to be right. If not, he'll fight you for it."

Of his own style, Walters later said: "I was a boxer. I wasn't a great puncher. I found that I could outbox anyone I fought. I never doubted that. I never went into a ring thinking that I couldn't outbox whoever I was in with. But.

Dave gives Canadian amateur champion and Olympic Games contender Len Walters last-minute tips before a fight. Although Dave was a more aggressive fighter himself, he recognized Walters' potential was as a more technical boxer. DAVE BROWN COLLECTION

To stand toe to toe? Every now and then I would stand toe to toe. Not do too good; 'OK, let's get back to basics.'"

Though Walters was sometimes criticized for not wanting to fight toe to toe, it was actually Dave who counselled him to jab and dance. When Walters didn't listen or Brown couldn't be in his corner, as was the case when Dave was suspended for punching out a referee in 1949, then Walters did "not do too good."

The occasion of the suspension was an event that Dave often recalls as "the time I punched the goddamned referee." As part of the preliminary selections for the British Empire Games, scheduled for Auckland, New Zealand in 1950, Dave, Walters and a middleweight named Jimmy Crooks went to Montreal. A deckhand on a Vancouver towboat, Crooks was not as gifted as Walters but was a hard worker who never complained about exercises or griped when he was asked to spar with an awkward newcomer. Dave liked Crooks, and wanted him to do well. In Montreal, Crooks was pitted against Toronto's Walter Dywan in a match refereed by Gaston Deschamps, a former stablemate of Dave's at Montreal's Crescent Athletic Club. During the first round, Dywan kept grabbing Crooks by the hips, clutching and holding. It was frustrating, and Crooks told Dave so between rounds. Dave recalls, "I told Crooks, 'Put your left hand out—measure him—and let go with the right. And he won't grab you any more.'" But when Crooks held off the clutching opponent, Deschamps warned him that a repeat would lead to disqualification. Crooks did it again, and Deschamps called him out for "illegal use of the hands." Victory, and the hopes of ticket to New Zealand, vanished.

Furious, Crooks went after Deschamps. Recalls Dave, "I jumped into the ring. Dennis White, who was national chair of boxing, said, 'You are going to get disqualified for this.'" I turned around and here's Deschamps—he's hitting Crooks with his bare fist. So I nailed him." A full-scale melee followed, with officials and boxers grappling in front of the bemused fans. The next day the BC team withdrew, citing Deschamps' behaviour as an example of the lousy refereeing that marred the tournament.

A cross-country war of words ensued, with the national Amateur Athletic Union and its BC counterpart arguing over the legitimacy of Dave's suspension. Despite repeated warnings from the union's eastern bureaucracy, he continued to coach and organize fights. The biggest of these was an event he planned for November, which featured Jimmy Crooks. Hours before the fight the AAU phoned and told Dave that if the fight went ahead, he and Crooks would be suspended for one year, starting immediately. If they cancelled, then the suspension was retroactive to the spring. The choice between the two meant that Dave could look forward to either six or twelve months of suspension. But hundreds of tickets had sold, and his fighter was ready to go, so he didn't have a choice. "With five months to tell me, they wait until the night of the fight after we announce the card with Crooks in the main event and received all kinds of publicity on it," he explained to a reporter. "Well, they can't get away with it, we won't let the public down."

For several months after the fight the BCAAU, which was on Dave's side, and the AAU argued about the duration of the suspension. Meanwhile, Walters, who had qualified for the British Empire Games, had to ship off without Dave. In Auckland, he won a bloody first-round fight, then lost a controversial decision in the semi-finals to the eventual winner, a South African with the unpleasant nickname "Smiler." E.H. Doherty, sports editor of the *Auckland Star,* decried the decision as one of the worst in Games history, and reported that "boos and jeers greeted the judges." But there was always the feeling that if Walters had had his long-time coach in the corner, things might have been different.

In the end, both Dave and Walters came out of the nasty affair amazingly well. Citing the Auckland decision as "a threat to the hegemony of the British Empire," Vancouver newspapers welcomed Walters, who returned without a medal, with more fanfare than if he had won gold. Forever after, the Auckland Games would be remembered as the time Walters got ripped off. Dave's suspension was resolved not by diplomacy but by practicality. At the January nationals in Montreal, the AAU discovered it didn't have enough regulation-sized boxing rings to accommodate all its events. In embarrassed desperation, it made Dave an offer: bring your boxing ring and reinstatement follows.

But Walters' best was still to come. After talking him out of a post-Auckland funk, Dave took Walters to Seattle for the annual Northwest Golden Gloves. The tournament featured a strong field of challengers, especially in Walters' class. Many fans predicted that the fight to watch was going to be between Walters and Jack Calvo, a top Seattle fighter. Calvo was known as an aggressive boxer whose windmilling punches destroyed more technical boxers like Walters. What they didn't know was that there was much more at stake for Walters. Prior to the fight, Dave had wrung a deal from the *Vancouver Sun*. At the time, the *Vancouver Sun* and the *Province*, then independent newspapers, were locked in a circulation war. The *Province* had just pilfered the *Sun*'s main publicity event, the Vancouver Golden Gloves. At Dave's suggestion the *Sun* started the Diamond Belt, which was open not exclusively to BC boxers, as was the Golden Gloves, but to top Western Canadian and Pacific Northwest boxers as well. A number of Vancouver fight clubs refused to participate if American fighters were allowed to enter. Dave thought the idea of limiting participation was stupid—in his opinion the more boxers, the better it was for the sport—but he saw an opportunity to get a favour from the newspaper. In return for Dave's boys participating in the Vancouver Diamond Belt, he made the *Sun* promise to pay the travelling expenses for one of his fighters to attend the Boston-based US nationals, the granddaddy of amateur boxing. All they needed to do to get to the nationals was win in Seattle. He had told his boys of the arrangement, and they had trained hard. Walters, in particular, had never looked fitter. He dispatched several challengers before meeting the much-touted Calvo. But if the crowd was looking forward to an extended three-rounder, they were disappointed. From the gong Calvo rushed Walters. Walters did some pretty footwork and uncorked a double left hook to the jaw. Calvo went down so hard that a doctor had to be called in.

What Dave had not counted on when he was dealing with the *Sun* was that not one but three of his fighters would qualify for the US nationals. Bobby Shires and Len Kupchak had won in Seattle as well. Dave took the matter to the *Sun* but the paper said it could only fund one boxer. Dave couldn't stand the idea of sending one of his fighters to the Nationals and not the other two, so he went to Vancouver police chief Walter Mulligan and asked if he could help convince the police board to raise money for a trip for all three boxers to Boston. They held a hugely successful fundraising fight card, and Dave and his boys were off.

In Boston, Dave and the boys booked into a hotel next to Boston Gardens, where the event was held, and scouted the competition. They had all been to big Seattle fights before but had never seen anything on the scale of the Nationals. The city had hosted the event for fifty-four of sixty-three years, largely because of the enthusiasm of its large fight-minded Irish-American population. Next to the Boston Marathon, the National Amateur Boxing Championships were the biggest single event in the city. And 1951, it turned out, was a banner year. Dick Tiger, Floyd Patterson, Gene Fulmer and Davey Moore were there; all subsequently became world champions in their various divisions. To add to the Canadians' bewilderment, besides the impressive quality of the American opposition, there was no fan support for the perplexed Canadians. Dave says, "When we arrived in Boston our cheering section would have got lost in a phone booth. It was composed of my father-in-law down from Montreal and another couple of fighters from Vancouver."

To win at the Nationals, a boxer had to fight five three-round matches in three days. Kupchak and Shires succumbed to good opponents in the early rounds but Walters advanced, beating two fighters, including a talented kid from Hawaii named Aladino Gusman. The toughest fight was his third, when he was pitted against Harry Smith of Canaan, New York. Earlier in the competition, Smith had beaten Davey Moore, a future world champion featherweight. Smith was a powerful boxer, with a good mix of technique and toughness. The two fought well in the first round, and Dave thought Walters might have a slight edge in points. But in the second round Smith spotted a hole in Walters' defence and knocked him down. Dave recalls: "My boxers were always taught to look into my corner if they go down. I give them the signal when to get up. The trick was to give them some time, but don't wait until it's too late—your body may not respond." Walters was on his feet before the count and struggled to finish the round.

Between the second and third rounds, Dave Brown crouched low and spoke in capitals to Walters. "I said, 'SON, YOU'VE GOT TO WIN THIS ROUND BIG. YOU'VE GOT ONE ROUND APIECE—BUT HE HAS THIS ROUND BIG—HE HAS A KNOCK-DOWN.'" Inspired, Walters fought what Dave considers to be his best round ever. He danced and jabbed and waited for opportunities. He snapped quick, hard punches, then slipped away before Smith could respond. When Walters got the decision the crowd at Boston Gardens rose to a standing ovation. Compared to that fight, the next was relatively easy. In the final, Walters met Gerry McGuigan of nearby Cambridge, Massachusetts, a crowd favourite. But no amount of encouragement could make up for the mismatch. Walter clearly dominated the first round, then,

The pain of Len Walters' controversial loss at the 1950 British Empire Games in New Zealand was erased a year later when he won the US Amateur Championships in Boston. The victory earned Walters an invitation to join a group of top American boxers on a European tour. Seated in the back of the car are (l–r): Sandy Brown beside dad Dave, Len Walters, Bobby Shires. DAVE BROWN COLLECTION

forty seconds into the second round, opened a cut over McGuigan's eye. The referee called the fight: a technical knockout. Walters was only the third Canadian to win the American National Amateur Boxing Championship. The victory earned him a trip to Europe with the touring American team.

A fierce competitor in the ring, Walters was almost shy about his accomplishments. On the night he was named Canada's amateur athlete of the year in 1951, Walters, then nineteen years old, was ringside at the Sunset Memorial Centre, cheering his fellow PMBA boxers. He drove home, switched on his bedroom radio, and heard the announcement. Several minutes later a reporter phoned and woke Walters' parents. They didn't even know their son was home. Later, when asked why he didn't wake his parents, Walters said he thought the news could wait. "They were asleep," he said. "I didn't want to disturb them."

Famous in Vancouver, Walters never disgraced himself with the kind of big-fish-in-a-small-pond arrogance that possesses so many successful athletes. He remained courteous to fans and friends and did his best to ignore the inevitable challenges from tough guys for street fights. "Maybe I had to defend myself once in a while," he says. "You're challenged. You defend yourself. A kick in the groin will do it every time." Unlike a lot of successful boxers, he did not think the sport was the sun around which the universe wheeled. As a professional, he once turned down the most lucrative fight of his career because it was scheduled a week before he was to be married. He didn't want to mar the ceremony with a black eye.

By 1952, Len was considered Canada's best hope for a medal at the upcoming Helsinki Olympics. He was twenty-one years old, superbly conditioned, fighting well. To get Walters to his peak, Dave had set him up as a sparring partner with the visiting Willie Pep, who was regarded as one of the best featherweights of all time. Pep needed the workout and was generous with his advice. After sparring for a few moments, he'd stop, tell Walters how he might adjust his style slightly, then resume sparring.

Dave and Walters arrived in Helsinki two weeks before the opening ceremonies. Boxing was slated for the last few days of the two-week event. In the weeks leading up to the fights Dave had Walters do his roadwork, spar, work out. The idea was to reach a peak the day of the fight, a readiness Dave describes as "boom, like out of a gun." The Games had many distractions, not least of which was the fact that Finland was nearly insolvent. Every day, big four-engined Condors wafted into Helsinki International loaded with bread from California. The change rooms were made of plywood, as were benches. Structural and organizational problems plagued the Games. Boxers fell through the ropes, one of the two rings collapsed. Over in the basketball courts, a fan, unhappy with a US referee's performance, disabled him with a kick in the groin. An English ref called off a heavy-weight fight because the challenger, the Swede Ingemar Johansson, wouldn't fight.

At first, things went well for Walters. Fit and rested, he easily won two matches and advanced to the semi-finals. But in his third fight he broke his hand on the head of a South African opponent. He finished the fight but was done for the Games. He says, "I took everything in stride in those days. I know I wasn't a shoot-off. If I won, I won. If I lost, I was robbed." He returned to Canada vowing to turn professional.

It is commonly heard in boxing that a fighter who

moves out of his division invites disaster. A boxer can move up but, it is said, "he can't bring his punch with him." It usually means that a fighter who will do well in a lower weight category may not be able to punch at the next level, but it also applies to a certain type of amateur who jumps to professional ranks. This was Dave's concern about Walters turning professional in 1952, and it is the reason he still believes that Walters' professional career was not more successful. Before Walters turned professional he and Dave made an agreement: if Walters lost two or three fights in a row, he'd retire. They had both seen too many boxers fighting long after they should have retired. Faces punched in, slow-witted, they were walking warnings of the danger of staying in the fight game too long.

In Walters' early professional fights, however, their pact seemed irrelevant. One of Walters' first opponents was Casey Jones, née Leroy Cason, of Portsmouth, Ohio. A former farmhand in Kentucky, Jones had been responsible for exercising Assault when that horse won the Kentucky Derby in 1946. He swapped leather saddle for leather gloves and was a rising star on the circuit when Walters put him away. After the Jones fight, Dave set Walters up with veterans Reuben Smith and Wee Willie Boyd. Neither boxer was as good a technical fighter as Walters, and Dave figured that Walters would win on points if he didn't knock them out, which was doubtful because he didn't have a punch that could flatten seasoned professionals. He was right; Walters was 3–0. Then he beat Teddy Hall, of Portland, in a remarkable match that saw Walters come back after a second-round knock-down. Afterwards, Hall said, "I never knew there could be that many fists in one ring at one time and all of them hitting you from every direction." A victory over Seattle merchant seaman Tony Alvarez followed. Alvarez said, "That Walters is uncanny. He always knows what you're going to do. You think you've got him but he isn't there." Things were looking good for Walters: he had a pocketful of money from his winnings and he had prestige.

Then, in blizzard-wracked Butte, Montana, things started to go wrong. Dave had arranged with long-time west coast fight man Sid Flaherty for Walters to fight Larry Vazquez, a spirited fighter from San Francisco. Flaherty, who would manage three world champions, thought the two boxers would make a superb match. Walters was a technical magician; Vazquez a firebrand. Dave agreed, convinced that Walters could win—he wouldn't have taken the fight if he thought otherwise—but only if Walters fought smart. That meant using the jab, dancing away and, most importantly, conserving his energy. As he had explained to Walters before, there was a big difference between a three-round amateur fight and ten rounds with a professional. A fighter who runs out of steam in the sixth round might as well stick his chin out and close his eyes.

Walters started in hard and stayed fighting hard until the bell ended the first round. In the corner Dave put his mouth near Walters' ear. "Lenny, you were beautiful. *What the hell were you trying to do?*" Panting, Walters said, "I had a good round, didn't I?" Dave said, "You had a great round, but can you go ten rounds like that?" Walters ignored Brown's warning and fought the second round like he did the first. As Walters towelled off between the second and third rounds, he told Dave he was convinced he could beat Vazquez. "I said, 'Horseshit. You know who is going to get stopped? You're asking for it, Lenny.'" Walters fought hard in the third and into the fourth round, then started to wobble. He made it out for the fifth round, but Vazquez knocked him down twice. Dave had told the referee that if his fighter went down twice he wanted the fight stopped. In the hotel after the fight, Walters peered through swollen eyes at Dave. "You're mad at me," he said. Dave said, "You didn't do what you were told. You fight a boxer and box a fighter."

According to the deal Dave made with Flaherty, if Walters lost there was to be a rematch in Vancouver, where the crowd—and possibly the judges—would favour Walters. After an easy match to rebuild Walters' confidence, the two boxers met in Vancouver. It was a good fight, with Walters boxing as Dave had coached, and he won a split decision. Flaherty, too, was pleased with the outcome and offered yet another match with Vazquez, but this time in Hollywood. Walters was all for the deal—Hollywood fights were getting national attention at the time—but Dave smelled a set-up. "I said to Lenny, 'We don't want it. You won't be the main event. You are a Canadian. Everything will be on his side. Do you want to buy a loss?'" Instead of simply turning down the offer and risk having Walters look chicken, Dave killed the deal by asking for too much money.

Walters, now 14–2, was next matched against Bobby Hicks, a Seattle puncher with an 8–0 record, seven of those knockouts. They fought at Vancouver's Exhibition

Gardens in February, 1956. For five rounds the two cir-
cled, Walters jabbing and moving away, Hicks patiently
seeking a knockout opportunity. In the sixth round, Hicks
buckled Walters' legs with a straight right, then followed
with a speedy, short left and another right. Walters was
laid out flat. He gamely got up before the count, but was
groggy and caught another punch—under the heart. With
Walters reeling, the referee called it off. A month later Len
lost to Jackie Moore in Seattle. Walters recalled, "All of a
sudden I had lost two fights in a row, which I had never
done in my entire life. Never. I decided to pack it in."

Any thoughts Walters had about returning to the ring
were wiped out several years later when he was involved
in an industrial accident while working as a pipefitter. He
was three storeys above ground when the scaffolding he
was on gave way. "I was going down face first," he
recalls, "and I got a chance to look up. The scaffolding
was coming down behind me. I managed to straighten
out and land on my feet." He broke fifty-two bones and
was on compensation for four years. Unable to return to
heavy work, he took a job repairing pay phones.

Dave and Walters remain friends. Len phones and
complains about his wife's swimming pool. Dave worries
for Lenny, as he still calls him, and hopes he is OK.
Walters named one of his sons David after his mentor.
Another son, Dale, inspired by his father's career, took up
boxing. In the 1984 Los Angeles Olympics he won a
bronze medal. Dale runs a glass-and-chrome boxing
exercise gym for the office set in the swanky Bentall
Centre in downtown Vancouver. For Lenny Walters' sixti-
eth birthday, son Dale videotaped an interview with Dave

in the Browns' front room. He gave Dave a microphone and said, "You know, Dave, you worked with my dad for thirteen and a half years. How would I have done with my dad?" Dave's answer was as reflexive as a counterpunch: "Are you *kidding*? Lenny Walters would have kicked the shit out of you."

Every boxing coach has a might-have-been-world-champion story; Dave's is about a good-looking young man with the kind of chippy, temperamental character that made things happen wherever he went. Buddy Pearson was a teenager when he walked into Dave's club in 1951, but he had the rounded shoulders and fully developed chest of an adult. Blond hair curled over his forehead and his quick eyes caught everything at a glance.

As Dave soon noted, Pearson had naturally quick hands, good balance and an incredible intensity. After several months in the gym, Dave let Pearson fight. He did well and advanced. Fighting as a flyweight, he won competitions in Vancouver and Tacoma. After several trips to Seattle, his gutsy fighting style made him the favourite of local fight fans there as well. At one Northwest Golden Gloves championship he convincingly knocked out a 126-pounder from the University of Washington, Steve Smith, in two rounds and received an ear-splitting ovation. His style was flat out, in the ring or out. In all, Dave took Pearson to the States eight times. Pearson won every time. "If he hit you, you were gone," Dave recalls. "He was game. He'd do anything to win."

As long as Pearson was fairly matched—as long as opponents were, like him, game and rising talents—Dave let them go. But as Pearson's reputation spread, fight managers south of the border put him up against cagier talent. In Seattle, Pearson was scheduled to fight Jackie Puskus. Puskus was a stocky fighter, who compensated for a lack of agility with a locomotive left punch and dirty tricks. He threw punches like pitchers throw fastballs: wide-open. He had been around the Northwest and to England, where he was disqualified three times for rabbit punches— innocuous little shots that curl around and hit the opponent on the back of the neck, temporarily disabling him. A rabbit punch is to boxing what high-sticking is to hockey. With a competent referee in the ring, a disciplined boxer could make his way past Puskus, who could be worked over on the inside, or his punches could be slipped. But Pearson wasn't disciplined. He was an explosion.

Dave told Pearson he couldn't fight because of his bad shoulder. "What do you mean bad shoulder?" replied Pearson. "You've got a bad shoulder. I'm telling the ref you can't fight. Son, if you wait six months, you'll play with Jackie Puskus. You're not mature enough yet. Right now you'd get your ass kicked in." Pearson accepted Dave's judgement, but grudgingly. Concessions weren't in his nature.

Out of the ring Pearson was always on the move, checking out the sunbathers at English Bay, hanging around matinees. When a friend suggested a joy ride to the Interior in a stolen car, Pearson decided to go along. They faked their way out of a citizen's arrest in Mission by pretending to have a gun and made it as far as Kamloops before a cop pulled them over. Pearson tried to do a James Cagney. "Look, asshole," he sneered at the cop, "I'll

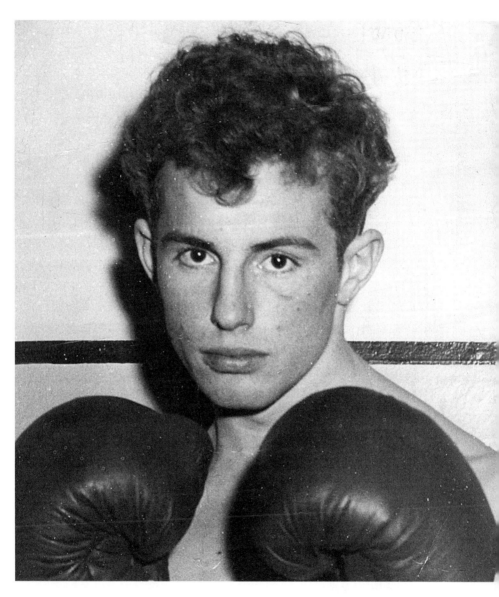

Handsome, athletic and a ferocious competitor, Buddy Pearson was the most purely talented of Dave's boxers. His promising career was cut short by a fatal neck injury. VANCOUVER NEWS HERALD

have you pounding the beat when I let Mulligan know about this."

Before Pearson's court date, Dave went to see the judge. He knew it wasn't usual, but in his mind Pearson wasn't usual, either. Given a chance, the kid might be able to straighten out. Dave explained to the judge that Pearson had had troubles and offered to vouch for the boy. The judge looked Dave in the eye and said that Pearson was getting six months definite, six months indefinite. After Pearson was released he seemed to be changed. He worked out at the gym, kept his probation appointments, stayed out of trouble. Then one day he strode into the gym wearing a new suit, new overcoat and the same old grin that Dave recognized as trouble. Pearson said he was going to a dance. "You mean girls?" said Dave. "Yes, girls," Pearson said. "Look: you are on probation," advised Dave. "Stay away from the girls. Do not get in any fights. Don't do any drinking." Before walking out, Pearson said, "You don't want me to have any fun at all." He was twenty years old.

It was the last time Dave would see Pearson alive.

Dave Brown was in bed that night when he got a call from Harry Twist of the RCMP. Twist was a boxing man himself and the two had a cordial if not close relationship. "Sorry I had to phone you, Dave," said Twist. "But Buddy Pearson got killed tonight." Brown, groggy, pressed the receiver to his ear and said "What?" The cop repeated himself but there was laughing in the background. What Twist was saying didn't seem possible. Now fully awake, Dave said, "Don't kid me about that, please." Twist wasn't joking. At the Keefer Street police station Dave rode the elevator to the third-floor morgue, two floors down from the PMBA gym. Pearson was under a sheet. There were no marks on the fighter's body.

The police invited Dave to question the kids the police had pulled in. They explained that Pearson had gone to the dance and got into an altercation afterwards. He was waiting with a girl when some guy made a remark about Pearson's hair. Never one to back away from a disagreement, Pearson said, "What are you going to cut it with, your nose?" A few more angry remarks, and the two were kicking each other. It wasn't any more violent than the average after-party fight. Suddenly, Pearson leaned against a nearby car. "Oh my god, I've had it," he said. Then he slumped to the ground, unconscious.

After the fight, Pearson's friends put him in the back of a car. They fetched ice from a Hastings Street restaurant and put it on his neck, but he didn't respond. Pearson was snoring raucously, what Dave calls "the old death rattle." The driver flagged down a cop on Kingsway. "You better have a look at the guy in the back," they said. "Something is the matter with him." The cop looked at Pearson and said, "He's dead."

At the coroner's inquest a jury heard from city pathologist T.R. Harmon. "There was a thickening of the membranes which was quite surprising in a boy this age," the doctor observed, adding that he had also found evidence of an old fracture and two hemorrhages. Technically, Pearson died from a blood clot in his brain, but there was no normal cause visible for the hemorrhage. "It could have been caused by excitement, sudden activities, or injuries," said the doctor. "Had it been removed I believe he would have lived." The jury's verdict was accidental death, but hovering around the inquest was a suggestion that the real culprit was boxing. The press twinned mention of Pearson's injury with his fight career in a way that left no doubt about the cause-and-effect link. It was possible, of course, but Dave felt it was improbable. Pearson was the type of boxer who administered beatings, not one who took them. In all the fights Dave watched, he'd only seen Pearson off his feet twice. On his own, after-hours, Dave mounted his own inquest. He discovered an event in Pearson's past that, to Dave, explained the fatal injury. Several months before Pearson had gone to jail he met some girls playing tennis on the Kitsilano courts. He put one of the girls across his lap and paddled her. She responded by taking a weapon at hand to the back of his head. She hit him on the exact spot where the doctor later identified the trauma. Buddy Pearson, the best boxer Dave had coached, was felled by a tennis racquet.

Chapter Six

Famous or obscure, every boxer has in his background a small fight of enormous consequences—an undercard loss that scotched an ascending career, a propelling small-town victory that caught the eye of a big-time promoter. It is the kind of thing fighters roll around in their mind for years afterwards, wondering what went amiss, or marvelling at good fortune. What is doubly strange about a fight that took place in December of 1946—a fight that had a huge effect on Dave Brown's career as referee and, later, professional judge—is that Dave was not one of the participants (he was not even in the building) and he barely knew those involved.

Outside Vancouver's Exhibition Gardens on that December evening, trolleys rumbled along the streets, their wheels raising a curious hum on the rain-slicked rails. A hard-driving southeaster was whistling through the city, and pedestrians clutched their fedoras, or fought two-fisted battles with umbrellas. It was an evening when the high ambition of all commuters was a hot tea and dry socks.

Inside the cavernous Gardens a different sort of gale was raging. Billy Townsend, not the McLarnin-era fighter but a round-shouldered, muscular boxer from Spokane, was methodically taking his opponent apart. Ace Carter, as he was announced to the crowd, had repeatedly borne blows to body and head in the first two rounds. Now, in the third round, his defences collapsed. With each resounding punch from Townsend, Carter's head lolled grotesquely and his arms flung to the sides. Helpless to defend himself, he looked like a man in the perpetual pose of falling backwards off a ladder. Finally, with his opponent dazed, Townsend lined up a hard right and laid Carter out cold. Not since Max Baer one-punched the Alberta Assassin had Vancouver's fight fans seen such a mismatch.

As a later police investigation into illegal betting revealed, Carter's skills were not all that was lacking in the card. Ace Carter was actually one Bomber Daniels, of Oregon. Three nights before the Exhibition Gardens fight, Townsend had destroyed Daniels in Portland. In the parlance of the ring, Daniels was a "ringer"—a fighter substituted under a name other than his own. Ringers have no hopes of going anywhere in the sport; they are boxing lunchboxers who remain for the meagre paydays. With an ear for made-up names, an unscrupulous manager can parlay a few ringers into a sizable stable.

At issue in the investigation was whether the promoter, Gene Mason, knew he was hosting a ringer. A small, neat man, with literary pretensions and an Ivy League manner of speaking, Mason was really a classic con artist with a thousand tricks for separating "pigeons," as he called the gullible public, from their cash. One of his simpler ploys involved an empty wallet seeded with a lucrative-sounding reward-if-found note and left on a sidewalk. Loitering nearby, Mason arranged to "discover" the wallet at the same time as an unsuspecting pedestrian, then brokered a deal whereby he agreed to forgo his share of the reward for a cash payout.

Mason had come to Vancouver after a bunco game in Alaska went awry and set up shop in a dingy apartment across from the Penthouse Club. Sleeping by day, he prowled the clubs during the evening, gambling on cards, dice, anything he thought would make an effortless buck. In summer, he ran a rigged booth at the Pacific National Exhibition. Customers thought they were paying for the chance to scoop numbered balls from a tank of water; if they netted one with a lucky number they won a prize. They didn't know that all the lucky balls were in an invisible trap, which Mason controlled by way of a hidden string. Searching for ever-easier ways to turn a dollar, he turned to staging professional fights.

When asked about the Townsend–Carter fight, Mason denied knowledge of any wrongdoing. He said he had contracted with Portland manager Larry Caputo for a fighter and Caputo had sent Carter. Yet Caputo claimed otherwise. He said he'd sent Daniels, as Daniels, and what strange metamorphosis occurred when the fighter crossed the border had nothing to do with him. Eventually it was revealed that Daniels wasn't really the ringer's name: Aso Clark, a.k.a. Ace Carter and Bomber Daniels, and of Who Knows Where, was actually a ringer for a ringer.

The situation was so bad—extending from promoters to boxers and big-time betting and, tangentially, into the Vancouver Athletic Commission—that Vancouver mayor Gerry McGeer became involved. A fearless reformer, McGeer had already taken on the Vancouver police during a corruption crisis in the 1930s and did not hesitate to include boxing in his latest scrub-up of the city. It didn't help Mason's nefarious cause that McGeer was a boxing enthusiast himself—the sprightly politician kept in shape by hammering a punching bag—and his speeches were shot through with boxing terminology, like "roadwork" and "people in his corner." During the spring of 1947 the problems in local boxing were McGeer's pre-eminent concern.

What investigators found was worse than even the most virulent boxing abolitionist would have dared suggest. Not only were ringers commonplace, but major gamblers had infected the local fight clubs as well. Some of the most damaging testimony came from long-time Vancouver bookie Louis Tisman, who submitted to investigators a 41-page hand-written genealogy of Vancouver corruption. Chief among Tisman's complaints was that a regular old-fashioned bribe, the kind that had once kept cops and officials from having too close a look at the fight game, no longer worked in Vancouver. With a kind of underworld outrage, he described how a newer, more moneyed set of gamblers were running the city's underworld—and professional boxing.

As a result of the testimony of Tisman and others, McGeer set about changing the way professional boxing was run in the city. He appointed a new Athletic Commission and implemented tough guidelines. Notice went out that the city's entire professional boxing scene— boxers, referees, promoters—were under a disciplinary watch. Though McGeer died before his reforms were fully implemented, their direction was set.

While McGeer's policies were flushing the system, another change was taking place among the small cadre of city boxing referees. For many years, Vancouver's premier "third man in the ring" was a small, cigar-chewing figure named Hector McDonald. A former amateur and professional boxer, "Phantom," as he was known, had 259 fights in Vancouver, California, and New York. When he retired from boxing in 1936, he took up reffing and became a missionary for the sport, entertaining the students at Vancouver College with stories about fighting in Madison Square Garden, or showing them how he kept his fight-swollen ears from swelling into cauliflowers by applying leeches. He was strong-minded, decisive, and respected. Yet even though he was just in his late thirties, McDonald suffered from a heart condition. By the late 1940s, he was finding it too difficult to work four- and five-fight cards and began to scout for help.

As a prominent member of Vancouver's amateur boxing community, Dave was an obvious choice. So they worked a deal to split the standard $40 refereeing fee. McDonald refereed semi and main bouts and pocketed $25; Dave took care of the preliminaries for $15. His attitude to refereeing was much as it had been in

Newfoundland: make sure no one gets hurt, encourage good fights and never, ever pay attention to the crowd. One of the first bouts he worked pitted veteran battler Kenny McPhee with an anxious-looking unknown from Kamloops. At the opening bell, McPhee strode to the centre of the ring and popped his opponent in the head with two quick unanswered jabs. On that evidence alone Dave called the fight. "The kid never moved a muscle. I just put my arms around him and led him back to the corner. The fans were shouting: 'Hey, Davey. What are you doing?' I'll always remember: there's one guy in the crowd; he says, 'Never mind. He knows what he's doing.'" The Vancouver Athletic Commission thought he knew what he was doing, too, and when Hector McDonald died in 1952, Dave assumed the role as the city's leading referee.

Like snakes fleeing a raptor, the unsavoury elements in the boxing community reacted to the changes in Vancouver by slithering off to outlying communities. But they still needed a credible referee and that's why an early professional boxing assignment took Dave to White Rock, where he worked a fight between Fran Porter and Ron Walley. The fight was held on a snowy December evening in the early fifties, in a half-full dance hall by the shores of Semiahmoo Bay.

Dave knew that the first people to get shafted on a poorly attended fight were the boxers, even if they were getting, like Porter and Walley, an unimpressive two hundred dollars apiece. So before the fight he asked their manager, Joe Martin, how the boxers were going to get paid. Confidently, Martin touched two fingers to his head, as if to say, "It is taken care of." Doubtful, Dave went ahead with the fight, even though there were no doctors or medical staff on site. It turned out to be a decent bout, with Walley winning an eighth-round TKO. Afterwards, while Porter and Walley anxiously awaited payment, Dave went looking for the suddenly absent Martin. He knew Martin was staying in a nearby hotel, so he paid the desk clerk to take a long look out the window and slipped in. Along the hallway he stopped at each door and listened; when he heard giggling and a familiar sounding voice he knocked. From behind a locked door, a female said, "Who is it?" Dave said his name and asked to be let in. The girl refused and Dave said, "Open the door or I'm going to knock the son of a bitch down." The door swung open; inside, Joe Martin, drunk, was sprawled on the bed; at a table, two young women were simultaneously working through a big jug of red wine and counting the gate receipts, which Dave could see were too meagre to include the boxers' payments. Nor did Martin mumble anything to make him think the money was forthcoming. Back at the hall, he told the two boxers to book into the hotel under Martin's name and not to leave until they were paid. It might take a few days, he said, but sooner or later someone will pony up. If there were any problems, they were to call. The ploy worked: the next morning the fighters were cut cheques.

On Dave's scale of boxing wrongs, the only thing worse than an irresponsible promoter is a slothful boxer. According to his equation, fans' time and money equals a boxer's skill and courage. A boxer needs to arrive at a fight in shape and with the right attitude. Otherwise, the fans get ripped off.

Refereeing a Seattle Golden Gloves match, Dave once stopped a fight because the boxers lacked enthusiasm. It was the final of the heavyweights and a capacity crowd had gathered at the city's Civic Center. Dave says, "Both guys were from Fort Lewis. They had made an agreement: you don't hurt me, I won't hurt you. They are weaving and ducking and bobbing. But they are *not* working at all. So halfway through the first round I open them up. 'Let's start fighting or I'm going to call this thing off.' At the end of the round I went to their corners and said, 'Look, you've had a round to warm up; start throwing some goddamned punches or I'm calling the thing off.' One corner guy says, 'You can't do that, man.' I said, 'Don't try me, sweetheart.' Halfway through the second round I said, 'Hold it—start fighting or I'll call this no contest.' They didn't bust their ass, so at the end of the round I called the announcer up. 'Call it off,' I said. 'No contest.'"

Disgraced in front of thousands of their fans, the boxers protested to the fight officials, who quickly summoned a meeting of all parties in front of Dick Francisco, then head of the Northwest Amateur Athletic Union. The boxers argued that Dave was biased and asked rhetorically if he would have stopped the fight if Canadians were involved. As Dave recalls, Francisco said, "Knowing this little guy for many, many years, had there been Canadians in there, he would have stopped it *earlier* than he did." That ended the meeting. Later, as Dave was preparing to return to Vancouver, Royal Brougham, sports editor of the *Seattle Post-Intelligencer*, clasped his hand. "This is a lesson that is going to last five years," he said. "These bastards have ruined more tournaments—especially in the final bout of the heavyweights. They get in there and dog it."

Dave eventually became one of the top-ranked referees in Canada. He worked scores of national-level bouts, including five heavyweight championships featuring George Chuvalo. Only the need to keep his job prevented him from accepting offers to work international-level fights. Francisco says: "Dave was one of the top referees in the world. He was better than he knew he was; he was world-calibre."

As a referee, it was Dave's job to decide what was in the best interest of the boxer, the sport, and the people who supported it all: the fans. The three constituencies did not always have the same needs.

Before dawn on a day that he was due to referee a heavyweight fight in Prince George, Dave got a phone call from Bob Wark, the Seattle manager of one of the scheduled fighters. Wark, still in Seattle with his boxer, wanted to know what road to take to get to Prince George. After Dave mumbled instructions, Wark told Dave that he'd had—"er, ah, ahem"—to substitute the scheduled heavyweight with another fellow. But, he added cheerfully, Dave was not to fret, the replacement was excellent. Dave recalls, "I said, 'Oh, yeah. What's his name?' I could hear Wark whispering: 'Psst—what's your name, kid?' I knew something was up." Dave advised Wark to take a hotel in Prince George and stay put until he flew in later. "I thought, 'If this guy gets to Prince George before I do he'll rob the town.' I'm no dummy. I know this guy."

Even in a sport known for its one-of-a-kinds, Bob Wark was an individual. Shaped like a bowling pin, and flashing two bleachers of tilting teeth, he was the sort of person of whom others said, "There will never be another like him." And for the health of boxing, that was probably a good thing. One Wark was all the sport could handle.

There are people in the small towns of southern BC and Washington who still recall the time Bob Wark arrived for a local card with a sedan full of ex-con boxers, three of whom were convicted murderers. During the 1950s and '60s he ranged from his dumpy Seattle gym across BC, Alberta and the US Northwest, hustling fights, squeezing an ever-changing clutch of boxers into one-light-bulb flophouses. His style was to travel light (all the better for après-fight getaways) and count on his considerable verbal talents to deal with events as they unfolded. Stuck for help in Ketchum, Idaho, Wark once talked a moon-faced old fight fan into working as his corner man. He didn't know Ernest Hemingway wrote books and he wouldn't have cared if he did. Hemingway could swab a glove-cut brow as well as anyone, and Wark made him a regular when he was in town.

Much of Wark's legend was based on his mouth, which, likes its operator, ran independent of orthodoxy. In a sweaty gymnasium crowded with Seattle's boxing elite he bellowed to the state's representative on the US Olympic Committee, "Open the window in here, will ya. It's getting sophisticated!" There were other stories, too: about his dealings with George "the Gorgeous Greek" Chemeres, the handsomest manager in all of boxingdom; or about the time he piloted an airplane full of sightseers

Whether he was refereeing a small-time amateur fight or a professional heavyweight championship, Dave discouraged clutch-and-grab-style fighting. Here he separates challenger Tommy Burns from cornered title-holder George Chuvalo. DAVE BROWN COLLECTION

into the side of the Bon Marché, in downtown Seattle. Miraculously, everyone walked away.

Dave Brown knew of Wark's exploits, too: "He had this guy in his gym, a good-looking light heavyweight. And he notices that every lunch hour some girls from the offices would stop and look him over. Whenever the kid saw the girls watching, he puts on a show; punches the shit out of the bag. Very impressive. So Wark manages to be standing nearby the girls and lets it be known that this particular heavyweight is a Canadian and very likely bound for the championship. And, as it happens, pieces of his contract were still available, at eight hundred dollars a share. The next day the girls handed over $800—or $400 each. Of course they never saw the boxer again."

In Prince George, Wark's fighter was in the second bout on the card. Looking at him beforehand, Dave thought he appeared tubby for a professional, but no more so than his opponent. For the entire first round the two fought as if magnetized: clutching and clinging to each other or, when separated, repelling to opposite corners, where they feigned angry looks and menacing gestures. Dave recalls, "At the end of the first round I told them to start fighting—start throwing some punches. The kid from Seattle says, 'I'm doing the best I can, Mr. Brown.' I said, 'Well, take a punch and keel over, because this thing stinks.' In the second round the other heavyweight misses with a left shot by about four inches—and this guy keels over. Down he went. That's what he did."

While Wark and his boxer slipped out a side door after the fight, a troop of befuddled local reporters descended on Dave. They wanted to know what had happened with the heavyweights. "They said, 'We didn't see anything. What happened?' I said, 'It was a short left hook.' You've got to say something."

Of his part-time career as a professional boxing judge, Dave Brown says:

"I judged seventeen world title fights for the World Boxing Council. I've worked with Julio Cesar Chavez, Martin Jabukowski, Kevin Patterson, Terry Norris. Norris knocked out Joe Gatti at the Alamo Dome, in San Antonio, Texas, in front of 65,000 fans. In the first round Gatti was down twice. He got to his feet and was hit through the ropes and fell on the apron and broke his nose. I got $1,800 for that one. I've worked in Korea, Australia, and all over the US, in Nevada, Texas, Connecticut, New Jersey, California. The only time someone tried to influence me was in Japan. Yuri Arvachako was defending his title. He was a Russian but trained in Japan. From the beginning things were weird. Somebody was supposed to meet me at the airport in Osaka—you know, with a sign "Dave Brown"—but there was nobody. I waited for a while and thought "Piss on it, I'll catch a plane home." Then this guy shows and says, "Mr. Brown?" and takes me to the hotel.

The night before the fight I'm in my room. I'm getting out of the shower and there's a tap on the door—very gentle. I answer and it's the front man for the pro- moter. He could speak English. A well- dressed man in his early forties was also there—he was the promoter. I said, "Wait until I dry off." They sat on the bed. The guy says, "We appreciate very much you coming from so far. I have an envelope so you can buy your wife a *beautiful* gift." I said, "Oh shit. I never did that and I don't intend to start now." I look over: the win- dow is half open, we are fourteen floors up. Both these guys are bigger than me. I said, "All I can promise you gentlemen is a fair, honest call. Good day." The front man, he got a little pissed off. His hair stood on end. He said again, "This could buy your wife a *beautiful* gift." I said, "I don't give a shit. I can't do it." So I told Marty Denkin, the ref from LA, about what happened and he said to forget it. Several months later I'm in Las Vegas to work the Terry Norris–Joe Gatti fight. I'm at the poolside at Caesars Palace, when José Sulaiman walks by. He's president of the WBC. I get a Christmas card from him every year. I told Sulaiman I was "approached." And Sulaiman says, "We know Dave Brown is an honest man," then he walks away.

> That's all he said. I still wonder if it was a
> test. I don't know.

For organized boxing's many critics, the only thing surprising about Dave's account is not that he was "approached," but that he didn't pocket the envelope— then ask for a free junket to Hawaii as well. Critics see the World Boxing Council and its organizational competitors in boxing, mainly the International Boxing Association and the World Boxing Association, as bad brothers in professional sport's most dysfunctional family. And as the largest of these organizations, the WBC often comes in for the most vigorous criticism.

The WBC was formed in 1963 out of a power struggle at the older WBA. A number of Mexican and Mexican-American fighters rightly thought the organization was weighing its rankings in favour of US fighters, and when the WBA refused to reform itself, they formed a rival organization with headquarters in Mexico City.

Since 1975, the WBC has been controlled by José Sulaiman, widely regarded as the most influential personality in professional boxing. A Mexican of Lebanese descent, Sulaiman was once a promising athlete, boxing as a youngster in the streets of Mexico City, then achieving some notoriety as a minor league baseball pitcher. He took over the family business and made a fortune producing specialized paper for medical instruments. Under Sulaiman's leadership, the WBC emerged from joke status to become the preeminent professional boxing organization that in the minds of many critics wields far too much power and not always in ways conducive to the sport's well being.

"You look into their eyes and see if they are all there," says Dave of how he determines whether a fighter is fit to continue after a knock-down. His first priority as referee was making sure a boxer was able to defend himself. Here he counts out a wobbly Tommy Burns, who has just been shelled by George Chuvalo. DAVE BROWN COLLECTION

Chief among the complaints is that the WBC fixes the ratings, elevating inept boxers controlled by favoured managers to coveted top-ten status, and relegating often talented boxers controlled by out-of-favour managers to ratings obscurity. Not only does this practice corrupt the sport, but it can lead to boxers taking part in horrifically mismatched fights. Bob Arum, a sometime manager wise to the ways of the WBC, is quoted in Stephen Brunt's book *Mean Business* as saying, "When we wanted a fighter ranked in the top ten we would talk to Mr. Sulaiman. Invariably he would put the fighter in the rankings." Still, acknowledged Arum, the WBC is better than its rivals. "José's at least trying to run his organization decently, to the extent that these guys know what decent is."

Dave knows of the WBC's problems. He has read of the rankings scandals. His response is not to deny they exist, but rather to work for the sport's betterment from the inside. Like a Catholic who chooses to remain with the church through its difficult times, he has stuck with the WBC from the first fight he judged for them in 1987, until ill health forced him to retire in 2000. For him, the fight is the thing; the bureaucracy is someone else's worry. So: is there corruption in the WBC? "Not that I know of. There probably is, but I've never seen it."

Dave was introduced to José Sulaiman in 1980, when he was covering the Roberto Duran–Sugar Ray Leonard fight in Montreal for radio station CJOR. Sulaiman knew Dave had refereed a number of Canadian title bouts, and asked if he might be interested in reffing for the WBC. At the time Dave had six years to go before retirement from BC Tel, and he knew the part-time demands of refereeing wouldn't go down well with his bosses. He declined, but took up Sulaiman's offer to work as a judge after he retired. In 1986 he was registered on the WBC's list of eligible judges, one of approximately two hundred worldwide.

A boxing judge is an art critic who renders his

opinion in numbers. If a fight is not decided by a knockout, the decision is passed to the judges. Throughout the fight they have been watching for what are sometimes called paramount criteria—effective aggressiveness, clean punching, ring generalship, quality defence. At the end of each round, they tally their points according to what's called a ten-point-must system. The winner of the round always gets ten points. If a round is a draw, both fighters get ten points. If there is a loser, that fighter gets a lesser number of points depending on his performance. At the end of the fight, their cards are tallied, and the result—win, lose or draw—is declared.

Dave's first assignment was the title fight between Carlos Zarate and Jeff Fenech, in Sydney, Australia in 1987. The fight had all the background that matchmakers look for. Zarate, a Mexican, was a remarkable boxer who had started his career by kayoing forty-four of his first forty-five opponents. Fenech was the hometown favourite, a classic handsome Aussie who on his days off did good deeds, like chumming around with a mentally handicapped friend.

The fight took place on an Australian spring day in November. For days the sports-crazy Australian press had built the fight to oceanic dimensions, and over seven thousand beery fans crowded into the suburban stadium. From the beginning, Dave says, "it wasn't a fight, it was a war." Zarate, a hard puncher, went straight to Fenech, who responded with well-timed counterpunches. It was fast and furious. At ringside, Dave kept a mental tally of the points. "Judges are not allowed to have a scratch sheet. None of that bullshit. It's all up here," he says,

Dave first met World Boxing Council boss José Sulaiman while covering fights for a Vancouver radio station. He later worked for Sulaiman as judge in 17 world title matches. DAVE BROWN COLLECTION

pointing to his head. "You can't be pissing around writing." Only when a round was finished would the judges mark their score cards and submit them for tallying.

According to Dave's interpretation of a judge's criteria, "If the fight was close, I always gave credit to the man who I thought was endeavouring to make a fight—understood? A good power shot to the chin, or a good power shot to the chest—it takes five jabs to level that off." For three ferocious rounds Zarate and Fenech battled. In the fourth round, while the two were fighting in close, Zarate staggered Fenech with a head butt. After inspecting the Australian fighter, the referee, Hank Elespora of Sacramento, California, called it off. The fans took the decision to mean that Zarate had won on a technical knockout and lurched from their seats towards the ring. What Dave knew and they didn't was that the WBC had recently altered its rules: if a deliberate head butt took place in the first three rounds, the boxer responsible was immediately disqualified. After that, it went to the score cards. As Dave and the other judges tallied their points, the crowd descended on the ring, angrily calling for the officials' heads. One fan, attempting to kill the messenger before he delivered the bad news, clambered over the judges in pursuit of the announcer. Dave recalls, "I told him, 'Look: Fenech was the buttee, not the buttor. Wait for the decision.'" He stopped his assault long enough to hear the call: a technical win for Fenech.

In February, 1989, Dave was holidaying in Hawaii when he received an intriguing call from the agent of a New York promoter. Former champion Roberto Duran was about to take on middleweight title-holder Iran Barkley in what promised to be the fight of the year. They needed a judge. If Dave could move quickly, the agent said, the job was his. Within hours, Dave was jetting east to Atlantic City.

Of Barkley, Dave knew little more than what he had

read in *The Ring* magazine, to which he subscribed. He kept back issues on metal shelves in his basement. Barkley was a brave all-round boxer, with a good jab, a strong if not devastating right, and a good chin. He was known as "the Blade," for the way he carved up opponents.

Of Duran Dave knew considerably more, in part because he had covered the Panamanian boxer's epic 1980 battle with Sugar Ray Leonard from ringside. At that time, Duran was regarded as professional boxing's premier ass-kicker—a fighter who didn't just beat opponents, but destroyed them. His style—relentless, vicious, bloody-minded—seemed barely removed from the ghetto dust-ups of his youth where, it was said, he once knocked a horse out with a single punch. After a lopsided victory Duran bragged that if he'd been in shape his opponent would be in the morgue instead of the hospital. Before the fight in Montreal he hoisted a middle finger at Leonard's wife and called her a *puta*—whore—and during the fight he spat in Leonard's face. He would, and did, do anything to win.

But Dave was also aware that things had not gone well for Duran after Montreal. Outboxed in a rematch with Leonard, he quit in the eighth round, famously muttering, *"No mas, no mas"* ("No more, no more"). Dispirited and boozy, he quit training and let his weight balloon. His career appeared nearly over when Wilfred Benitez hammered him in 1982, and a fifteen-round loss to Marvin Hagler a year later seemed to be the end. By 1984, he was an embarrassment to himself, pummelled flat by Thomas Hearns in two rounds. When he disappeared from the ranking charts, it was widely regarded as good for professional boxing. As *Sports*

Illustrated's Bruce Newman said, the only thing that seemed to lie ahead of the once-great Duran was his paunch.

Then that phenomenon that galvanizes so many supposedly has-been boxers to return to the ring happened to Duran: he ran out of money. Whether it was caused by a fleet-footed manager, or the fighter's preference for many, many of life's (usually single malt) treats, did not matter. Duran was broke. Slowly working himself back into shape, he took on a series of no-names until he was once again in a position for a lucrative title challenge.

This was the background story as Dave took his ringside seat with the other judges at Donald Trump's swanky Atlantic City Convention Center. In the champion's corner Barkley, a superbly conditioned, technically adept boxer in his prime; in the challenger's corner Duran, thirty-seven years old, a retreaded once-great brawler willing to do anything to succeed in a comeback.

With the largely Hispanic crowd cheering for Duran, Barkley began the fight by going for his opponent's midriff. Duran slipped many of the blows, but Barkley persisted, leaning into his punches and tracking Duran across the ring. Duran settled into the centre of the ring, where he threw nasty jabs at the circling, ever-moving Barkley. That set the pace until the end of the sixth round. In the seventh round, Barkley changed tactics and stunned Duran with a whistling hook to the head. As the bell sounded, the two stood glaring at each other. What had started off as a boxing match had turned into a fight.

Barkley scored again with the hook in the eighth round, several times sending Duran weaving across the ring. Though the fight was close, Dave had Barkley ahead on points. He liked Barkley's persistence and thought Duran's style too off-and-on. In the eleventh round, Duran hit Barkley with three devastating combinations. Barkley finessed his way through the first two but, with his eye swelling shut, got caught on the third and sat on the canvas. He recovered and wobbled around the ring until the bell. Both boxers fought ferociously in the twelfth and final round.

Without a knockout, the decision was up to the judges. While Dave thought Duran had won several of the later rounds, he had Barkley ahead overall on the strength of his earlier performance. He submitted his twelfth-round points card and awaited the results with the rest of the crowd. The result stunned Dave and a number of observers: a split decision in favour of Duran. According to Dave, before the fight one of the other judges reportedly said, "If Duran doesn't win there will be a riot." Dave says, "He was scared shitless. So he went overboard for Duran."

Though voting for Barkley did not make Dave popular with pro-Duran fans, it earned him a lot of respect in the wider boxing community. "It's easy to go along with the idols in these kind of fights," says Don Majeski, a New York-based boxing adviser and thirty-year veteran of the sport. Commending Dave's dissenting decision, he notes that a panel of independent judges overwhelmingly favoured Barkley. "[Judges] make bad decisions, not out of corruption, but because they get caught up in the mood of a superstar. Duran and Barkley was a very big fight. But if you took the emotion out of it, turned down the sound, you'd say Barkley won."

Chapter Seven

In Dave Brown's mind, boxing is a neighbourhood without streets. For all his adult life he's had at least as much kinship, often more, with fight enthusiasts as with the families flanking the cedar fence bordering his property. Of the members of this unique sporting precinct, he will say, "we speak the same language."

Good-natured Earle Kalani spoke Dave's language. Part native Hawaiian, the cherubic Kalani was, a friend once remarked, "as nice a guy as ever tossed three thousand bucks to the seagulls." He came to Vancouver from Detroit, where he'd been a member of Bing Crosby's band, and opened a motel. He got into promoting because he loved boxing and stayed with it because he was stubborn. His first promotions, in 1953, lost money, as did all but nine of the twenty-eight bouts he staged over the next four years. He blamed television for Vancouver's ever-diminishing crowds; with international-level fights broadcast weekly on *Gillette Friday Night*

Fights, boxing fans couldn't be bothered to pay for live shows featuring local professional talent, like brothers Frankie and Stan Almond, Kenny McPhee and Bill Brenner.

Yet even when Kalani arranged for big-name appearances something always seemed to go screwy. A much ballyhooed bout between Murray Burnett and Harry "Kid" Mathews from Seattle was disrupted by a record-setting rainstorm. Another time he contracted with former heavyweight champion Max Schmeling to referee a local fight, only to have Schmeling cancel at the last moment in favour of a speaking engagement with the Chicago Germania Club. When Kalani did finally sell out a card it was only to belatedly discover that the ticket takers had undercharged their friends.

In 1957, Kalani reached deep into the pockets of his big, loose-fitting suit to fund a promising fight between South American heavyweight champion Eduardo Romero and Joey Maxim, former world light heavyweight champion. Both were respected, hard-hitting fighters with reputations for going flat out from the opening bell. Romero, known to national television audiences, had also fought in one of the few money-making professional fights in Vancouver, several years earlier, when he took on an up-and-coming Canadian fighter named Earl Walls. Though outclassed as a boxer, the ox-like Romero had waded through a barrage of punches to wear Walls down. The gate for that fight was a sizable (for that time) $25,000.

For small-time promoters, the risk of bringing in an out-of-town boxer is that there is no way of judging his condition. A fighter's record may look impressive, but is ultimately no sure indication of his current fight-readiness. So Kalani had no way of knowing that Romero and Maxim were out of shape until they waddled off the airplane. "They come to town looking like two fat old women and I was dead as soon as folks got a look at them in workouts," recalled Kalani. "They even had to wear sweatshirts on TV so viewers couldn't count the rolls of fat around the midriff. I was never so disgusted in my life."

In the days leading up to the fight Maxim, at least, acted like a serious boxer: impressively pounding the heavy bag during training, making the traditional pre-bout predictions about how he was going to maul the South American. The porcine Romero, though, did not look like a boxer and he did not behave like a boxer. Childlike in his innocence, he mistook the advances of two hookers as a sign they were hungry, and stood them for triple ice creams. The boxer's trainer decided to have some fun with his charge, who did not speak English, and taught him to speak a sort of upside-down language—down for up, left for right, yes for no—so Romero lived in a state of relentless irritation.

With plenty of bad publicity, the Romero–Maxim fight drew a measly crowd that grossed $4,700—about $3,500 less than it cost Kalani to stage. Writing in the *Province*, Eric Whitehead called the much-touted fight the "floperoo of the century" and begged the unfortunate Kalani to pony up another $100 for Airwick to clear the post-fight atmosphere.

Dave knew first-hand of Kalani's bad luck. When Dave was managing Len Walters' pro career, Kalani came looking for an opponent to match against an undefeated lightweight. At the time Dave was looking for a featherweight opponent for Walters; it turned out they could help each other: Kalani knew of a suitable California boxer managed by George Chemeres and Dave had just reacquainted himself with a lightweight looking for a fight. Dave first met Blaine Hayden while refereeing an annual boxing card at the BC Penitentiary. There were many good fighters in the institution, and among them Hayden was a standout, with quick hands and the kind of natural balance that many fighters struggle for years to develop. When Hayden was released from jail he came to Dave looking to turn professional. Dave saw enough potential to take him on.

The card was scheduled for a Saturday at the PNE Gardens, on Hastings Street. Dave arrived early for the afternoon weigh-in, then paced the sidewalk awaiting Hayden, who sauntered in twenty minutes late. He made weight, then Dave invited him home for dinner. After gulping his meal, a fidgety Hayden said he had to fetch his coat. "Coat?" said Dave. "It's seventy degrees, for Chrissake!" But Hayden was strangely adamant; he needed his coat.

As billed, Hayden was to fight a semi-final with George Chemeres's lightweight. Again, he arrived late and barely had time to change before the fight began. He dominated the first round, flattening his opponent with a fantastic combination of punches. Shortly into the second round, however, the two boxers went down in a tumble and Hayden got up complaining about his shoulder. Sensing something whiffy, Dave said, "I hope you're not kidding, because I don't want to lose my licence. You understand me?" After Hayden's feeble performance in the third round, he was convinced. He told the referee he was going to get a doctor to look at the boxer's shoulder. It was a poor showing in yet another card that lost Kalani money.

While Dave was at work the next day, Hayden appeared at the Brown home. He looked remarkably healthy, with a new suit, a fancy car and a pretty girl. More surprising still was the wad of cash he handed a somewhat shocked Phyllis; as he explained, it was repayment for money Dave had lent him. He told Phyllis he could have won the fight but had arranged to throw it instead. Prior to the match he had ex-con friends lay bets on 8–5 odds that he wouldn't go four rounds. "I made more money than the whole card," Hayden boasted.

Despite losing money year after year, Kalani always thought that, given the right combination of boxers, the somnambulant Vancouver fight scene could be turned on. His final effort, in 1957, was aimed at organizing a fight featuring Archie Moore, the great and durable American light heavyweight. It was Dave who put Kalani on to Moore. Like a lot of other boxers, Dave admired Moore as much for his tenacity as for his skills. When Moore was in Vancouver for an exhibition, he would train at Dave's gym in the Patricia Hotel; they were friends. Dave was talking to Moore on the phone when Moore suggested that he would be interested in defending the light heavyweight championship of the world in Vancouver if—and it was a big if—he was guaranteed $75,000.

Dave wasn't interested in promoting a fight himself, but Kalani thought Moore might draw a big crowd. Kalani set about organizing the fight; he made preliminary arrangements with Moore and booked Capilano (later Nat Bailey) Stadium as the venue. The kind of crowd a Moore title fight would draw wouldn't fit in any building; it had to be outside, and that meant it had to be in August when the weather was good. As the fight approached, Dave encouraged Kalani to stay in touch with Moore, who was notoriously up and down in his weight. Finally, with the fight just weeks away, Moore confessed that he wasn't going to make weight for August and said he wanted it rescheduled for October. Disillusioned, Kalani backed out (he died soon afterwards), and two eastern businessmen matched Moore with Canadian Yvon Durelle in a fight at the Montreal Forum still widely regarded as one of the best ever in Canada.

Journalist Archie McDonald and broadcaster Al Davidson were good at mimicking the language of the boxing community, but during the 1970s and '80s, when they wanted the inside story they talked to Dave. He always had friend-of-a-friend accounts, the kind that an announcer could wedge in when he had an hour of vacant air time and no guests. "Davidson would call in a panic and tell me to get down to the station," recalls Dave. "I could talk forever." Headphones clapped on his ears, he yakked with callers about the local fight scene and professional rankings—always adding an insider's contrary gossip. Of promoter Don King, the sport's most controversial figure, Dave says, "Don King is the best promoter in boxing; he pays $40 a day in meal allowance. That was enough for Phyllis and I to live on. Before a fight he used to give me the thumbs up; he didn't do that for anyone else." To the inevitable questions about George Chuvalo—Was he Canada's greatest-ever heavyweight? Was it true that his punches lacked knockout crunch?—Dave responded with stories about refereeing a brutal heavyweight fight in Penticton, when Chuvalo destroyed an opponent who headbutted him.

Even if he didn't have the inside story, Dave was always good for a quote, and his name gave a sports article credibility. And the more his name was in the paper, the greater his credibility. Archie McDonald was a young reporter with the *Vancouver Sun* in 1963 when he came up with a nifty story idea. Jack Dempsey's former trainer had just published an account of how he applied plaster of Paris to Dempsey's hands before his epic title fight with Jesse Willard in 1919. With hands like cement, Dempsey won, and changed boxing history. McDonald thought they might put the account to a test themselves. Dave taped McDonald's hand as if preparing for a fight, then applied plaster of Paris over the tape. When the application hardened, Dave held a metal trash basket against a wall and McDonald punched it into scrap. Dave got his name in the paper and McDonald got his story.

Dave's sister Isabell was prominent in local sports, too. An outspoken woman, with wide-set eyes, an engaging smile and the determination of an icebreaker, Isabell had seen how few activities there were in the 1960s for her severely disabled son, Tim. She set about altering that situation with the kind of single-mindedness that Dave brought to boxing. It made people think that their seemingly endless energy was genetic. Isabell created the Burnaby Athletic Club in 1973, and developed programs to train mentally handicapped people in sports and recreation. In 1980 she and her husband Roy Cavallin founded what has since become one of the strongest sport-governing bodies in the province, the BC Special Olympics. She coached track and field, soccer, swimming and bowling. Her athletes competed at local, regional, provincial and national levels. For her work, she was named to the BC Sports Hall of Fame in 1996.

Through his work as coach, referee, commentator and later chair of the Vancouver Athletic Commission, by the late 1970s Dave had become a sort of man-about-town celebrity. His name appeared in Jack Wasserman's gossip column, or the sports pages. He liked the attention and never lacked opinions on the fight scene. Only now and then did the publicity backfire. Off work on a compensation claim, Dave was riding along Commercial Drive with Roy Cavallin one day when they spotted a purse-snatching. The crook, a tall, rough-looking guy, dashed down a side street and Cavallin swung his car after him. Halfway down the block they cut him off. Dave, donning his trademark "don't try me, sweetheart" look, stepped out, opened the car's back door, pointed, and said, "Get in, asshole." As the suddenly remorseful crook explained, he had only taken the purse because he was hungry. On the way to the police station, Dave spotted the woman whose purse had been stolen, and Cavallin wheeled up to the sidewalk. The crook apologized, but in doing so managed to explain his circumstances in such painful detail that his recent victim rooted an apple from her purse and gave it to him. Her generosity got to Dave and Cavallin who decided jail would do the fellow no good, and they sent him on his way with all the pocket change they could muster—fifty cents each.

According to a story on the front page of the next day's newspaper, however, the innocent purse snatcher turned out to be a seasoned con with five aliases. Police caught him drinking beer in the Waldorf Hotel with Dave and Cavallin's dollar. The story included all the details of the celebrity catch-and-release, which led to a horrendous ribbing from Dave's friends ("Fifty cents, Dave? *Fifty* cents?"). His bosses at BC Tel read the account, too. "They saw the story in the paper and phoned and said, 'We think you better come back to work tomorrow. If you are good enough to be catching robbers you are good enough to work.'"

Former heavyweight champion Rocky Marciano spoke Dave's language. The two developed a fast and strong friendship in 1967 as a result of a phone call Dave got earlier that year from a local chapter of the Shriners. The Shriners thought they'd like to bring Joe Louis to town for a fundraiser and wanted to know if Dave could make the arrangements. Yes, Dave said, he could, but then added his own thoughts. He had seen Joe Louis speak in Seattle and was left with the feeling that it was a good thing Joe Louis didn't go into broadcasting. Besides, he said, Louis's wife handled his affairs, and she was notoriously prickly. Dave recalls, "I said, 'Why not bring in a colourful guy. I can get Rocky Marciano. He's not black, but he's pretty close to it.'"

In the mid-1960s, Rocky Marciano represented to about one half of the boxing world the eclipsed greatness of the sport. A decade earlier he brawled his way to the heavyweight title deploying a punch called the Suzy-Q, then won an amazing forty-nine fights, forty-three by knockout. He retired undefeated and began a second career as a public speaker.

From his boxing contacts, Dave knew Marciano had three homes—in New Jersey, Massachusetts and Florida. Dave tracked him to Fort Lauderdale, and Marciano said he was interested. After several days of negotiations, Marciano agreed to five days' work in Vancouver for $3,000, plus prepaid airfare. Then Dave started working his many media contacts to build up the visit. Nory Finlayson, Dave's former navy captain, now in charge of Seaboard Advertising, donated prime billboard space in downtown Vancouver. The newspapers picked up the story and ran advance features. A week before the fight, Marciano phoned from New York and said he was heading west to California and would make his way north to BC. With days to go before the fight the phone was ringing constantly in the Brown home: Bill Good Sr., Ted Reynolds, Erwin Swangard—the ranking sports journalists of the day—were eager for stories and wanted to know when Marciano would arrive. Exasperated, Dave phoned Marciano's brother in California; he said Rocky wasn't there, but that he had said to pass on the word that "everything was all right." When Dave inquired further he discovered the ex-champ was making his way—bumming

Dave had admired Rocky Marciano's bulldog ring style but found the retired boxer's obsession with his hairpiece irritating. Dave escorted Marciano, working a second career in public speaking, around Vancouver for a week in April, 1967. DAVE BROWN COLLECTION

a plane ride here, freelancing a speaking engagement there—on to San Jose, San Francisco and Tacoma. The travel money was safe in his pocket. With time running short, Dave tracked Marciano to the Olympia Hotel in Seattle. "Don't worry," said the former champion, "I can

In Dave's opinion Rocky Marciano was a lousy referee—the former champion officiated at several Golden Gloves fights when he visited Vancouver and was awkward in the ring—but he could draw a crowd for a fundraiser. Marciano is seated second from left, Dave third from the right. DAVE BROWN COLLECTION

run from here." Dave had public relations events lined up for Wednesday afternoon. When Marciano said he'd arrive at about 4:30 p.m., Dave cut him off. "Bullshit," he said, "you are coming in the morning."

All Wednesday morning Dave fretted. Finally, after lunch, Marciano called to say he was arriving at 2:20. "I was shitting myself," Dave says. "There were all these reporters who wanted to talk to him. They kept saying, 'When is he going to get here?' I said, 'You'll get your story. Just hang on.'"

Marciano wasn't what Dave expected. "He wasn't as

tall as he was supposed to be," says Dave. "He was about 5'10" and had a toupée. He was always fitting the son of a bitch." Despite the schedule problems, Dave and Marciano got along well, Dave says: "We spoke the same language." Marciano had a sort of friend-of-everyone rep- utation, but privately told Dave there was one guy in the fight game he didn't like. At a press conference years before, Sugar Ray Robinson had mangled his name—as Marciano said, "trying to make me look like some sort of a wop off the boat." Only his managers had kept him from going after Robinson right there. And Marciano was sure he would have pounded him: "Dave," he said, "you know as well as I do that a good big man will always beat a good little man."

As Marciano's twenty-four-hour escort, Dave was at his side during the luncheons, dinners and ceremonies. He accompanied the former boxer to the Hotel Vancouver, was ringside when he refereed Golden Glove bouts at the Agrodome. Everywhere they went, Marciano was followed by reporters and fans. One night after he and Marciano had gone to their respective hotel rooms Dave heard a woman working her way down the hall, knocking on doors, and calling, "Rocky, Rocky, let me in." As Dave lay in his hotel bed, he heard a door open. When he met Marciano at breakfast the next morning he winked and asked how he had slept. The boxer said "fine" and looked at him oddly. Then another member of the entourage came to the table, a grin on his face. He had heard the woman calling Rocky's name, opened his hotel room door and said, "Yes? Can I help you?"

Jack Cohen did not speak the language of boxing, but he was willing to buy a lunch to hear someone who did. The prosperous owner of Vancouver's Army & Navy stores, Cohen liked to bet on heavyweight fights, but only if he could get an insider's point of view. During 1959 and the early 1960s, when the heavyweight title was ping-ponging between Floyd Patterson and Ingemar Johansson, Dave's insider knowledge helped Cohen go an impressive three for three on his bets. Before the first fight the betting was on Patterson, in part because of Johansson's pathetic showing at the Helsinki Olympics. But Dave had been in Helsinki and understood that the moody Johansson had been unwilling rather than unable to fight. Furthermore, he knew that Johansson had been working in New York's legendary Stillman's gym and was much better than widely thought. He told Cohen he liked the look of Johansson; the Swede took the title. Meeting over burgers before the second Patterson–Johansson fight, Cohen wondered whether he shouldn't bet on the champion again. As it happened, Dave had just been in Seattle, where he'd chanced upon Archie Moore in the washroom of the Olympic Hotel. Moore told Dave that Patterson had been invigorated by the defeat; his neck size had increased, he was in superb shape. Dave told Cohen he liked the look of Patterson; again, Cohen collected. Dave predicted Patterson's next win over Johansson, too. The next time Cohen saw Dave and Phyllis shopping at Army & Navy, he waved them by the cash register with a wink.

Like Cohen, Don McIntyre relied on Dave's insider

knowledge of boxing. During the 1970s and '80s, McIntyre and Dave worked on the five-member Vancouver Athletic Commission, which supervised professional boxing in the city. "Dave operated very much as the man who knew everything and we respected that," says McIntyre, a former school principal. "He'd say: 'This guy is a bum, this guy is a joker, or, this is a mismatch.' He was opinionated but very knowledgeable."

That knowledge was especially useful when the commission, which included Roy Nosella, Bob Gatto and city councillor George Puil, was deciding whether to grant a fight licence. On paper, a promoter might satisfy the commission's notoriously high standards for deposits, doctors and facilities, but without an intimate knowledge of boxing it was hard to tell the legitimate from the hocus pocus. One time the manager for Nanaimo boxer Shane Sutcliffe made a long and eloquent pitch to the commission and followed it up with a video presentation of his boxer's victories. When it was over, Dave said, "Why didn't you show us the fight he lost in Kamloops?"

An oft-used ploy by promoters is to push the deadline for meeting requirements until the last possible moment. By that time advertising and word of mouth has built public expectations and any decision to end the fight is blamed on the commission. The VAC rarely flexed to such pressure, but there were often some very tense late-night decisions. Says McIntyre: "Dave gets pretty excited—he would order us around as if we were joe-boys. He would phone Bob and call him 'Roy,' then phone Roy and call him 'Bob.' Then he would tell Bob what an asshole Roy was and tell Roy what an asshole Bob was." When the other commission members, who genially accepted the comments as part of the Dave Brown package, told the commission chair of his mistake he'd scoff, "You guys don't know what you are doing." Says Dave: "I don't want to be chucking the shit too much. But. They were not— N-O-T—boxing men. They didn't know a left hook from a button hook. Do you understand me? So they depended on me."

Appointed to the commission in 1972, Dave was chair and chief spokesperson for twenty-three years. Under his watch, the VAC introduced stringent medical and health requirements and reduced the number of ringers by tapping into a New Jersey-based computerized tracking system. He wasn't popular with promoters, but his efforts made Vancouver the international standard. "It should be the model for every commission in the world," says New York's Don Majeski. A thirty-year veteran of the business, who has worked on fights in Australia, Asia and North America, Majeski says the VAC's insistence on getting cash in advance has helped it avoid the fight-and-scram type of promoter. "If American commissions were run the same way everyone would walk away happy."

In 1996 Brown advised the commission that ill health was going to force him to resign. George Puil, the city's representative on the commission, told him: "Damn it, Dave, you can't quit. You *are* the commission. This is ridiculous, you've done a wonderful job."

Some of the VAC's toughest decisions involved the so-called Tough Guy fights of the late 1970s and early 1980s, in which unskilled, exuberant young men battled in the

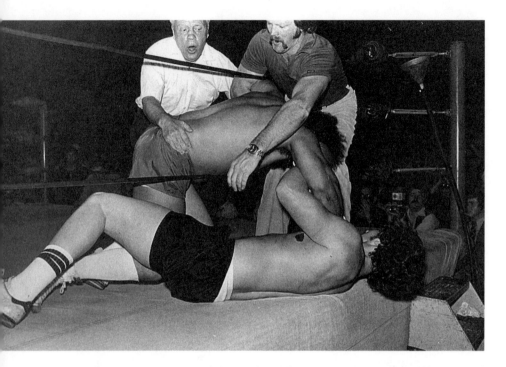

What So Ya Wanna Fight and similar promotions of the 1970s and '80s lacked in sophistication they made up for in bar-room-style spontaneity. Here Dave helps manager Tony Dowling pull boxer Gordy Racette off an unidentified opponent who blindsided Racette after Dave called the fight. DAVE BROWN COLLECTION

ring. To fans of traditional boxing, So Ya Wanna Fight and similar productions like So You Think You're Tough? were aberrations, the sort of popular eruption that, like karaoke, ruined a beautiful thing by handing it to the philistines. The flailing fists and ungainly moves of the truckers, housemovers and drywallers were a final affront to a sport that had long honoured skill, training and discipline.

SYWF was brought to Vancouver by Jack

McLaughlin, a sometime promoter and owner of a Hastings Street music store. The fights had been going on in the East for at least a year, and when McLaughlin saw an SYWF-style card broadcast on television he thought it might do well on the West Coast. A few posters, some media stories, and the first fight was ready. The phenomenon, if that is what such a rough-and-tumble event can be called, lasted off and on for a decade.

The popularity of SYWF was simple: give the working man a chance to box. Racing schools had been giving aspiring Jackie Stewarts the chance to turn a high-speed lap, so why not boxing? Furthermore, boxing was popular. Canadian Shawn O'Sullivan was on his way to winning a gold medal at the World Cup; *Raging Bull* and *Rocky* were playing in theatres.

At first, Dave and the VAC were cautiously optimistic about the Tough Guy fights. In spirit, they were a healthy throwback to the days of old-time fighting and it seemed they might rejuvenate the city's moribund boxing scene. As long as the organizers provided the usual security— medical staff, deposit money—they were granted permits.

Furthermore, the VAC had an inside source on what was really happening in the fights: Dave refereed them. The chance to make some money with their fists was especially appealing to professionals who, for one reason or another, were out of boxing. One heavyweight who had suffered what Dave calls "a bit of brain damage" tried to climb in the ring. "I know all about you," said Dave, and threw him out. Another fighter was almost blind. Dave didn't recognize him until he was blinking across the ring. Out he went.

But the very success of Tough Guy-type fights was their undoing. As the prize money increased, it attracted a better calibre of boxer, and fights became increasingly lopsided. Fights that used to last all three rounds were, by the early '80s, now being finished in one. Two boxers especially, Jerry "Mack Truck" Reddick and Gordy Racette, dominated their weight categories. When the entire VAC went to watch a card and saw Mack Truck knock an opponent out in the first round they decided to end that type of boxing in Vancouver.

In their set-up, the SYWF events were a throwback to the days when a bush league system brought up the best fighters. What the promoters were hoping for was a contender, someone who could burst from the ranks. From the melee of SYWF one fighter emerged who went on to have a noteworthy career.

Dave was impressed with Gordy Racette the first time he saw him fight. "He was a big, good-looking white kid. With the right training I thought he could be in the money in a couple of years." Raised on Vancouver Island, he had the kind of enthusiasm that seemed ideal for a fighter. Racette was a star rugby and lacrosse player, known for his immense strength and hard playing style. He played hockey, took a black belt in karate. When he wasn't working part-time as a bouncer, he took home-study courses in camouflage and weaponry. His goal was to become a professional bodyguard.

In 1978, at the age of twenty-three, Racette entered and won a series of So You Think You're Tough? competitions, many of them refereed by Dave, on Vancouver

Island. Dave thought Racette had talent but wasn't ready for true professional-class opponents. He thought Racette would benefit from more local fights. It was Dave's intention to let Racette develop for another year, then approach him about going professional. But an ex-fighter beat him to Racette. Tony Dowling put Racette through a crash course in boxing basics, and in 1980 introduced Racette to the professional boxing world as "Canada's new heavyweight sensation." Dowling was involved peripherally with the SYWF and had seen Racette's potential. "Canadian heavyweights are so bad you can win the title with a letter from your mother," he said. Dowling, a cagey manager, and one-time member of the French Foreign Legion, pitted Racette against a hapless Mike Silva. Racette knocked him out in one round, then a month later did the same thing to John Hagen. In the next three months Racette racked five more first-round knockouts—proof, in the opinion of many fans and journalists, that Canada's Great White Hope was legitimate.

But there were skeptics, Dave among them. To pit a well-built brawler like Racette against quarter-time opponents was one thing. But to set him up with a journeyman professional boxer was another test—and if Jimmy Young was anything, he was experienced. In 1976 he lost a close fight to Muhammad Ali, and a year later beat George Foreman so badly the former heavyweight champion retired. (He came back a decade later.) But Dowling was convinced of Racette's abilities. In a one-sided fight in front of Racette's Nanaimo fans, Young stopped Racette in ten rounds. Four pick-me-up wins followed, and Dowling pitted Racette against Trevor Berbick for the

Canadian heavyweight title. The fight was halted in the eleventh round, after Berbick had knocked Racette halfway out of the ring.

Under Dave's rules, Racette would have gone back to bouncing. In nine months he had lost badly to two world-class opponents; he was outclassed and in his late twenties. But an offer came along from a moneyed American movie star that neither he nor Dowling could refuse.

Ever since he had made the popular boxing movie *Rocky*, Sylvester Stallone had hoped to turn up a real-life boxer to fit the description. He hired Richie Giachetti, an associate of boxing boss Don King and former trainer of Ernie Shavers and Larry Holmes, to scout. At first Giachetti turned up Lee Canalito, an earthmover-sized fighter with a 40–0 record. Everything was ideal—except that Canalito couldn't win against quality opponents.

While scouting the boxing hinterland, Giachetti saw Racette take an impressive ten-round decision from Scott LeDoux, in the fall of 1982. In Hollywood style, things then happened very quickly. Stallone phoned Racette, and soon Racette and Dowling were on their way to California. Dowling was soon ditched—with a reported $40,000 to ease the exit—and Racette was signed on with Tiger Eye Productions. As part of the deal, "Canada's heavyweight sensation," as he was announced to the West Coast press, was given a leased Jaguar and an apartment.

Unfortunately for Racette, that was as good as it got. When he fell out with Giachetti, Stallone hired Ray Notaro to look after the training. Racette won several unremarkable fights, then lost an important fight to Tony Tubbs.

The potential that Vancouver Islander Gordy Racette (left) showed in Tough Guy–type fights was never realized when he turned professional. In Dave's opinion Racette was moved up the boxing ranks too quickly by, among others, actor Sylvester Stallone. DAVE BROWN COLLECTION

After that, things started to go wrong. "Sly made me a bunch of big promises that he never kept; in fact, he never kept many of his little promises, either," Racette later said. "It got to the point where I couldn't even get new boxing boots from him."

Racette returned to BC vowing he was finished with boxing. He attempted a comeback in 1991 but after a couple of hopeful-looking performances was obliterated in two rounds by then Canadian champion Conroy Nelson.

Chapter Eight

In 2000, Phyllis Brown was striding along the seventeenth fairway of Kensington Pitch and Putt, in Burnaby, when she turned to check on her husband. Playing with Dave at least once a week, and often more, she had come to expect his duffer's pace—the dawdling walk, the unhurried kibitzing with strangers. What she saw this time, however, was his prone figure. He was face down on the grass.

Dave had already been diagnosed with Ménière's disease—a mysterious affliction of the inner ear. It has many symptoms, including headaches that have been described as one hundred times worse than a hangover. Such descriptions don't mean much to Dave who, with stoic joviality, makes light of his condition to visitors. Even in his youth, he says, he was a two-beer man. "I was a cheap drunk." In the mid-1980s he quit drinking altogether. He's proud of this and announces it often. He may as well have given up second-hand cigarette smoke. But the incident on the golf course signalled another stage of the disease.

Because he never knows when an "attack," as he calls the periods of dizziness, will occur, he cannot travel easily. This has forced him to turn down judging assignments for the WBC, but given the state of boxing that may not be such a bad thing. The last fight he was asked to judge was the light heavyweight match in the fall of 2000 featuring Canadian Davey Hilton, who at the time was accused of sexually assaulting two girls. Hilton was later convicted but in 2001 was appealing the decision.

Now, from his comfortable position on the beige couch, with the chiropractic stuffy wrapped around his neck, Dave acts as a clearing house for both family and old boxers. His four daughters live nearby; all are married and have children. Sandy and Brian Kask's children, Brian and Debbie, are involved in Curtis Lumber Company, the family construction supply business. (A large-sized print featuring Dave refereeing the Ali–Chuvalo fight hangs in Brian Jr.'s office.) Brian Jr., married to Stephanie, has three children: Kaila, Kassidy and Ryan (whom great-grandfather Dave is successfully lobbying to have called "Rocky"). Dave and Phyllis's daughter Heather and her husband, Gerry Meech, have three children: Kyle is married and lives in Maple Ridge; Kelly is in the second year of a hockey scholarship at Wayne State University, in Michigan; and Michael is in the first year of a hockey scholarship at Brown University, in Providence, Rhode Island. Vicki, married to Peter Respondek, has children Adam and Lisa. And daughter #4, Lori, and husband Jeff Eppler are raising Jenna and Anthony. The entire family,

The Brown's daughters and their families turned out when Dave received the City of Vancouver Civic Merit Award. Back row, standing (l–r): Gerry Meech, Michael Meech, Debbie Carella, Jeff Eppler, Kyle Meech, Stephanie Kask, Brian Kask Jr., Peter Respondek, Brian Kask. Middle row, standing (l–r): Vicki Respondek, Heather Meech, Sandy Kask. Seated, (l–r): Jenna Eppler, Kelly Meech, Phyllis Brown, Dave Brown, Lori Eppler. Front row (l–r): Anthony Eppler, Lisa Respondek, Adam Respondek. Not pictured: Great grandchildren Kaila Kask, Kassidy Kask and Ryan ("Rocky") Kask. DAVE BROWN COLLECTION

now extending to four generations, is remarkably free of rift. The daughters, separated by what once seemed a generation-sized age difference (Sandy and Lori are seventeen years apart), are friends. Dave and Phyllis have often travelled to Hawaii with Brian and Sandy and they've holidayed with their other children as well. A recent trip saw Dave and Phyllis jet to a Barbados resort with the Epplers. One morning, as the family was heading out for a day of sightseeing, Dave decided he didn't have the energy to carry on. The adults were considering who was going to remain with Dave when grandson Anthony piped up. "I'll stay with you, Grandpa," he said, and the two returned to the resort. That sort of generosity of spirit is incredibly satisfying to Dave and Phyllis.

Dave keeps track of the remaining members of his boxing club, too. Len Walters, retired nearby, calls to complain about the hassles of maintaining a summer home in Birch Bay. "He's a good kid," says Dave. In the spring of 2001, former PMBA boxer Norm Jorgenson was overcome with an urge to visit his old coach. "I don't know; I just had to see Dave," he recalls. Now in his sixties, Jorgenson and his wife drove to the Brown home. Episodically, they recalled the old days: of how Jorgenson had to train for a year ("A year!" says Jorgenson) before Dave would let him fight; of the time Jorgenson won the Canadian welterweight championship in Regina. Jorgenson had come to Dave's club a dedicated street fighter—a hard-minded youth who loved knocking kids down, then beating them some more. Through Dave, he found in boxing discipline and focus for his energy; after his first session he never fought on the streets again. These were the things they talked about that day in Dave's home. When it was time to go the two men, old boxers now, but firmly aware of life's round, stood face to face at the Brown's front door. Recalls Jorgenson, "I said, 'I love you, Dave.' It choked him up, you could see. But it's a fact."

Hugh Meikle, whom Dave calls Hughie, also stays in touch. Meikle, now retired from a job as an electrical inspector, joined the PMBA in the mid-1950s, after arriving from Scotland via a brief stay in Detroit. A Scottish youth champion, he was trained in the formal, upright British style, then learned to bob and weave in Detroit. In Vancouver his father made repeated inquiries about boxing instructors and was always given the same name as the best in town. He walked into Dave's gym and saw fifteen fighters working out—half of them Canadian champions. The place reeked of achievement. "Dave put a polish on me," says Meikle. "I had a big hammer of a left hook. I knocked a lot of guys out with Dave."

Like Dave's other boxers, Meikle recalls their coach as a high-energy guy who could have a good time just getting to a match. "He'd be driving and turn around to talk to a guy in the back seat. We'd say, 'Jesus, Dave. Watch where you're going!' And he'd say, 'OK, OK. And keep on talking.'" At the Canadian amateur championships, in Regina, Dave allayed the worries of Meikle, who thought he might not make the weight limit, by stopping a cop in the middle of a prairie downpour and asking if he knew where he might find a weight scale. As it turned out, a friend of the cop owned a pharmacy. "They opened the store and before long Dave was bullshitting with them like they were all old-time friends," Meikle recalls. Relieved that he was going to make weight, Meikle focussed on the task at hand, and won the Canadian featherweight title.

According to Meikle, the thing that made Dave a winning coach, as well as a fun coach, was his ability to befriend his boxers. He knew about their home lives, and was willing to listen to their problems. An arm around the shoulder of a forlorn boxer was just as much a part of the Dave Brown system as shadow boxing. Then, when the intensity of a fight was at its greatest, boxer and coach had a unbreakable bond. "If you were in the third round, Dave could give you that little advantage. There was no way I could spell the word 'lose'." Meikle says, "We always felt good when someone said, 'Who's your coach?' And we'd say, 'Davey Brown.'"